TAOS 1847

THE REVOLT
IN CONTEMPORARY ACCOUNTS

Edited by
Michael McNierney

D1557811

Johnson Publishing Company : Boulder

For Carolyn

ISBN: O-933472-07-2

Printed in the United States of America by
Johnson Publishing Company
1880 South 57th Court
Boulder, Colorado 80301

CONTENTS

A Missouri Mounted Volunteer
(Hughes, *Doniphan's Expedition*, 1850)

I. Introduction

Late in the afternoon of 18 August 1846 the Army of the West entered Santa Fe. To one observer, the town was "an irregular cluster of low, flat roofed, mud built, dirty houses," appearing "more a prairie-dog village than a capital." The population watched the ragged lines of *Americanos* file past the Stars and Stripes, raised for the first time above the plaza. The women covered their faces with their hands or sobbed aloud. Most expected to be branded on the cheek with the "U.S." they saw on the soldiers' sabre belts.

A few months after the first skirmishes of the Mexican War far to the south near the mouth of the Rio Grande, Brigadier General Stephen Watts Kearny had marched 856 miles in less than eight weeks to capture the capital of New Mexico without firing a shot. For him, it was the first and an important step toward California.

The troops appreciated the magnitude of the occasion somewhat less than did their commander. After a thirty-mile march through intermittent rain, they pitched their tents on the barren hills outside the town. The early ground afforded no forage for the horses, and wood and water would have meant a walk of several miles in the dark. Thirsty men and horses bedded down on empty stomachs. A private in Doniphan's regiment remarked sarcastically in his journal that "having witnessed the dawning glory of New Mexico . . . we went to sleep to dream off the dull cares of a soldier's berth. So ends the glorious eighteenth."

The Army of the West was an anomalous formation. Five companies of the U.S. 1st Dragoons, Kearny's regiment, formed a backbone of regulars for the 1700-man force. Two companies of artillery, two of infantry and a detachment of topographical engineers provided some tactical flexibility to the command.

But the majority of the troops consisted of the 1st Regiment of Missouri Mounted Volunteers, raised at President Polk's request for the purpose of capturing Santa Fe. What would later be called mounted infantry, the volunteers were not trained as cavalry, indeed were not trained at all. They were good shots and their courage and self confidence (mainly a boundless sense of superiority over the "greasers") were never in doubt, but their discipline left everything to be desired. Once the Missourians came into contact with Turley's famous "Taos Lightning" they were uncontrollable. Their hatred and contempt for the *Nuevo Mejicanos* would cause problems for as long as they, or their successors, Col. Sterling Price's 2nd Missouri Volunteers, remained in the territory.

For several days prior to the entry into Santa Fe, rumors had been flying through the Army of the West that Governor Manuel Armijo had entrenched 7000 men in Apache Canyon through which the Americans had to pass. Armijo was, in fact, determined to fight at first and had deployed 200 regulars and 2000 militia in the defile.

But before Kearny reached the canyon, he received a welcome message from Acting Governor Juan Batista Vigil y Alarid. The messenger blurted out a concise summary of its contents from his mule before handing the letter to the general: "Armijo and his troops have gone to Hell and the canyon is clear." Armijo, after discovering that few of his officers were willing to fight, decided that discretion is the better part of valor and headed for Chihuahua with ninety dragoons as a body guard. His army dissolved.

Acting Governor Vigil welcomed Kearny to Santa Fe. During the next few days the general assured the inhabitants that the new government would protect their lives, property and religion. He absolved them from their allegiance to Mexico and officially announced the annexation of New Mexico to the United States. A man of intelligence and tact, Kearny did his best to smooth over relations with the conquered people, respectfully attending Mass and giving a ball to which both Americans and New Mexicans came. His actions seemed to allay some of the inhabitants' fears which had been exacerbated by propaganda making the gringos out to be rapacious monsters.

Kearny moved quickly to bring American law and government to the conquered territory. Under his supervision, license fees for businesses were established and a law code prepared. On 27 September the general appointed Charles Bent territorial governor.

Bent was one of the proprietors of Bent's Fort up on the Arkansas and a well known trader in New Mexico. He had kept a residence since 1832 in Taos where he had attained minor political prominence. Though he had enemies in the powerful Martinez family, led by Padre Antonio Martinez, he also had friends in high places. Bent had been on good terms with Kearny for some time. On hearing of the projected invasion, he had hastened to Fort Leavenworth with Ceran St. Vrain to consult with Kearny.

Peace reigned for the moment in New Mexico, and General Kearny was anxious to be on to California and the second half of his mission. Accordingly, he set 25 September as the date for his departure with the 1st Dragoons. Colonel Doniphan was to take the 1st Missouri Mounted Volunteers to Chihuahua to join General Wool once he was relieved by Colonel Sterling Price and the 2nd Missouri. Kearny calculated that Price's regiment, Clark's artillery and Angney's batallion of Missouri infantry would be sufficient to garrison the pacified territory.

On 6 October Kearny's column met Kit Carson below Socorro. The scout brought news that California was under control, so Kearny sent all but two companies of the dragoons back to Santa Fe before proceeding west.

Once the American presence in New Mexico was weakened by Kearny's and Doniphan's departure, trouble which had been brewing beneath the surface for some time broke out. Many New Mexicans quite naturally felt humiliated by Armijo's disgraceful rout and intensely resented the rowdy and insulting behavior of the occupying troops. Some members of the upper classes were disappointed that they had not received positions in the new government and hoped to obtain by revolution what they failed to acquire by cooperation or silence. The leaders of a revolt could reasonably expect the support of the lower classes. Food and other supplies were scarce due to the disruptions of war, a condition not improved by the

3

presence of a hungry and ill supplied occupying army. Everyone, high and low, who held land, feared they would be dispossessed by the invaders. Wild rumors of Mexican victories to the south only served to add urgency to hope. During the third week of October, the army picked up information about a possible uprising. Mild martial law was enforced in the Santa Fe area, and the troops were kept on the alert as well as poorly trained volunteers could be. While Mexican and Indian rebels trained secretly in the hills, correspondence addressed to former Governor Armijo requesting aid from the south against the widely scattered American troops was intercepted on 20 November.

Thomás Ortiz and Colonel Diego Archuleta led the band of conspirators which also included members of the Pino and Armijo families of Albuquerque and several clergymen. The beginning of the revolt was planned for 19 December with the murder of Colonel Price and Governor Bent but was moved back to Christmas Eve when the leaders thought that it would be easier for a large number of people to gather without arousing suspicion.

But someone informed on the conspirators. Precautions were taken instantly, most of the leaders were arrested, and the plot collapsed. The outnumbered Americans breathed a sigh of relief, and the ease with which the "greasers' " plans were thwarted reenforced the invaders' sense of their own superiority.

Governor Bent, for one, was convinced that the danger was over. Though intelligent and experienced, he had an unrealistic view of his own acceptance by the Mexican-Indian community. With a few friends, and refusing the offered escort, he made the difficult winter journey from the capital to his home in Taos to visit his family. After living in New Mexico off and on for twenty years, it was simply inconceivable to him that his adopted people would harm him.

Near dawn on 19 January 1847 a band of Mexicans and Indians led by Pablo Montoya, "the self-styled Santa Ana of the north," and Tomasito, the leader of the Taos Indians, crept through the silent, star-lit streets, converging on the governor's house. They kicked in the door, and while the sleepy governor tried to talk them down, scalped and killed

4

him. In his last few seconds, Bent must have realized the truth learned by victims of all revolutions: that the hatred of the down-trodden for the privileged runs far deeper than the gloss of familiarity and good intentions.

That night and the following day five other Americans were butchered in Taos, and more at Turley's Mill (Arroyo Hondo), Mora and other outlying areas. That the Taos revolt was totally unexpected is the strongest indication that it bore no direct connection with the earlier, aborted plot in the Santa Fe area. Proof, however, one way or the other is lacking. Clearly, both rose out of the same atmosphere of frustration, smouldering resentment and wild rumor.

At Santa Fe Colonel Price learned of the murders on 20 January and reacted quickly. With a company of volunteers recruited by Ceran St. Vrain to supplement his small force, Price marched northward on 23 January with 350 men. Only St. Vrain's volunteers had horses. After defeating the insurgents at several places on the snow-choked way to Taos, Price reached the village around noon on 3 February. Finding that the rebels had taken refuge in the church of the pueblo three miles away, he decided to attack immediately, although his men were exhausted from the hard march and winter fighting. After two hours of ineffective bombard-ment, the Americans retired to the village at the approach of darkness.

The next day, following more work by the artillery, the troops successfully stormed the church. St. Vrain's men, posted on the opposite side of the church, cut off the fleeing defenders. The revolt at Taos was over.

Of the two judges who subsequently tried the rebels, one was a close friend of Charles Bent, and the other's son had met a particularly horrible death the night of Bent's murder. The jury, composed partly of friends and relatives of the slain men, repeatedly announced, to no one's surprise, verdicts of guilty and sentences of death. In fifteen working days between the fifth and the twenty-fourth of April, fifteen out of seventeen men were convicted of murder, one out of five for high treason and six out of seventeen for larceny. The executions for murder were carried out on an improvised gallows with borrowed lariats and tether ropes.

Rebels and raiding Indians kept the outlying areas in an

uproar for most of the year. The army maintained a temporary force at Taos until October 1847 when it was decided that the unstable conditions demanded more permanent arrangements. Three companies of the 3rd Missouri Mounted Volunteers were accordingly ordered to garrison the official "Post of Don Fernando de Taos."

Never again did rebellion break out at Taos, though on several occasions political violence seemed imminent. Eventually, however, Taos residents looked to the U.S. Army for protection against raiding Utes and Apaches. The military which had been the object, and sometimes the cause, of so much animosity, came to be tolerated as a necessary part of the community—useful for defense and a convenient market for local produce.

But the Taos Revolt was long remembered, both by the defeated and by the victors. The documents collected here present the events of 1847 strictly from the point of view of the latter. The rebels were mostly illiterate and disorganized, and, except for some court testimony, few written records exist from their side.

Still, the following accounts present the revolt from a variety of perspectives. They range from the memoirs of a mountain man, dictated many years after the events in which he participated, to official reports written a few days after the action and dispatches sent almost before the smoke of battle had cleared.

Perceptive readers will notice, or suspect, contradictions and overstatements, mistakes and truth-stretching. Memories are distorted by grief, hatred, ambition and blatant racism. The motives behind the creation of even the simplest document were sometimes varied and complex, but seldom was the primary purpose objective reporting.

But for a sense of immediacy and a glimpse into the minds of the participants in historical events there is no substitute for first-hand accounts. The purpose of this book is simply to gather together in one place as many accounts as possible of this episode in the Mexican War which was almost immediately overshadowed by the much larger scale events in Mexico.

II. The Murders at Taos and the Fight at Turley's Mill

1. Charles Bent to James Buchanan

Santa Fe, N. Mex., *December 26, 1846.*

Sir:

I have been informed indirectly that Col. A. W. Doniphan, who, in October last, marched with his regiment against the Navajo Indians, has made treaty of peace with them. Not having been officially notified of this treaty, I am not able to state the terms upon which it has been concluded; but, so far as I am able to learn, I have but little ground to hope that it will be permanent.

On the 17th instant I received information from a Mexican friendly to our Government that a conspiracy was on foot among the native Mexicans, having for its object the expulsion of the United States troops and the civil authorities from the Territory. I immediately brought into requisition every means in my power to ascertain who were the movers in the rebellion, and have succeeded in securing seven of the secondary conspirators. The military and civil officers are now both in pursuit of the two leaders and prime movers of the rebellion; but as several days have elapsed, I am apprehensive that they will have made their escape from the Territory.

So far as I am informed, this consipiracy is confined to the four northern counties of the Territory, and the men considered as leaders in the affair can not be said to be men of much standing.

After obtaining the necessary information to designate and secure the persons of the participators in the conspiracy, I thought it advisable to turn them over to the military authorities, in order that these persons might be dealt with more summarily and expeditiously than they could have been by the civil authorities.

The occurrence of this conspiracy at this early period of the occupation of the Territory will, I think, conclusively convince our Government of the necessity of maintaining here, for several years to come, an efficient military force.

  •   •   •   •   •

C. Bent.

Hon. James Buchanan,
 Secretary of State of the United States.

2. U.S. Government Proclamation—Santa Fe, 15 February 1847

On the 13th of January, 1847, Charles Bent, governor of the Territory of New Mexico, left Santa Fe, the seat of the government, for Taos, his place of residence. While there the friends of two Pueblo Indians who were confined in the prison at that place requested him to release them, to which he replied that, although governor of the province, it was entirely out of his power to release anyone confined by law until they were tried. They then resolved to release the prisoners by force and murder all the Americans in Taos, together with those Mexicans who had either accepted office under the American Government or were favorable to Americans. On the Tuesday following they effected their resolution, releasing the prisoners and barbarously murdering and scalping Governor Bent; Stephen Lee, sheriff; James W. Leal, circuit attorney; Cornelio Vigil (a Spaniard), prefect; Narcesses Beaubien, and Parbleau Herrmeah, sparing but one American, named Elliott Lee. Leal was scalped alive. At the Arro Onlo, 12 miles from Taos, the following men fortified themselves in a house, and after standing a siege of two days were taken and murdered: Simeon Turly, Albert Cooper, William Hatfield (a volunteer), Louis Folque, Peter Robert, Joseph Marshall, William Austin, Mark Head, and William Harwood. The number of Mexicans and Indians engaged in this massacre has been estimated at 300.

3. From Colonel Sterling Price's Report to the Adjutant General—Santa Fe, 15 February 1847

About the 15th of December last I received information of an attempt to excite the people of this territory against the American government. This rebellion was headed by Thomas Ortiz and Diego Archuleta. An officer, formerly in the Mexican service, was seized, and on his person was found a list of all the disbanded Mexican soldiers in the vicinity of Santa Fe. Many other persons, supposed to be implicated, were arrested, and a full investigation proved that many of the most influential persons in the northern part of this territory were engaged in the rebellion. All attempts to arrest Ortiz and Archuleta proved unsuccessful, and these rebels have, without doubt, escaped in the direction of Chihuahua.

After the arrest above mentioned, and the flight of Ortiz and Archuleta, the rebellion appeared to be suppressed; but this appearance was deceptive.

On the 14th of January, Governor Bent left this city for Taos. On the 19th of the same month, this valuable officer, together with five other persons, were seized at Don Fernando de Taos by the Pueblos and Mexicans, and were murdered in the most inhuman manner the savages could devise. On the same day, seven Americans were murdered at the Arroya Honda, and two others on the Rio Colorado. The names of the unfortunate persons thus brutally butchered are as follows:

At Don Fernando de Taos.—Charles Bent, governor; Stephen Lee, sheriff; James W. Leal, circuit attorney; Cornelio Vigil, (a Mexican,) prefect; Narcues Beaubien, (son of the circuit judge;) Parbleau Harvimeah, (a Mexican.)

At the Arroya Honda.—Simeon Turley, Albert Turbush, William Hatfield, Louis Tolque, Peter Robert, Joseph Marshall, William Austin.

At the Rio Colorado.—Mark Head, William Harwood.

It appeared to be the object of the insurrectionists to put to death every American and every Mexican who had accepted office under the American government.

9

4. Dick Wootton's Account

In the fall of 1846 and in the early part of the winter of 1847, I was in and out of the old town of Fernandez de Taos, very frequently, but was fortunate in not being there at one particular time.

That was when the Mexicans stirred up the rebellion, which culminated in what has always been known as "the Taos Massacre."

In August of the year 1846, General Kearney had gone into Santa Fe, with the body of troops which he had marched across the plains from Fort Leavenworth, and had taken possession of the capital of New Mexico, as well as other towns through which he had passed on his way to that point, without opposition.

The Mexicans had taken the oath of allegiance to the government of the United States, and New Mexico was looked upon as a conquered and subjugated province. General Kearney then proceeded on his way to California, leaving Colonel Stirling Price, with a few companies of troops at Santa Fe. Colonel A. W. Doniphan came through from Fort Leavenworth with another body of troops later, and also stopped at Santa Fe.

Aside from the small force of soldiers stationed at Santa Fe, and possibly small detachments at Albuquerque, and one or two other places, I do not think there were any troops left in New Mexico, when Kearney pushed on to the Pacific Coast.

For a time both the Mexicans and Indians professed to be very friendly, and the Americans got along well in New Mexico. By and by, however, it was noticed that a considerable number of the Mexicans were for some reason becoming dissatisfied with the condition of affairs, and Colonel Price, who was in command at Santa Fe, found it necessary to keep a close watch on their movements. It was not long before he discovered that Tomas Ortiz and Diego Archuleta, two prominent Mexicans, had set on foot a plan to bring about a general uprising of the Mexicans and Pueblo Indians. They were to act in concert, and at a certain time were to fall upon all the Americans and other foreigners in the territory, and either kill or drive them out of the country. The Mexicans didn't seem to have much of an idea of the size of the contract they were undertaking, and the Indians, of course, were led on entirely by the Mexicans, who promised them an easy victory and plenty of plunder. This scheme was discovered in time to be nipped in the bud, and Archuleta and Ortiz left the country to escape punishment.

There was nothing like a general uprising at that time or even after that, but a Mexican named Pablo Montoya and El Tomacito, an Indian, concluded some time afterward, to go ahead with the proposed rebellion on their own account. They gathered together a considerable force of natives, and marched to Taos, on the night of the 18th of January, 1847.

As I have already told you, Fernandez de Taos, or Taos, as we always called it, for short, was a Mexican town, having a population of five or six thousand people.

The Pueblo de Taos was an Indian village about two miles from the town. It consisted of one large Pueblo building, six or seven stories high, and a church, which stood some little distance away, both built of adobe.

I suppose there were something like a thousand Indians in the Pueblo. It was at this point that the Indians and Mexicans met, to commence their march to Taos, and the slaughter of the foreigners, of whom they proposed to rid the country.

There were not more than fifteen white persons, or perhaps, properly speaking, persons who had no admixture of Spanish or Indian blood in their veins, living in the town of Taos, and several of these happened to be absent from their homes on the memorable 19th of January, 1847.

Those who were at home, when they got up in the morning, found the town surrounded by as merciless a band of savages as ever went on the war path, and they quickly caused it to be understood, that their intention was to kill every white man, woman and child in the place.

Charles Bent, who had been appointed military governor of New Mexico, by General Kearney, lived at Taos, and had come up from Santa Fe, which was of course his official headquarters, only a day or two before. His residence was one of the first places attacked, and he was butchered in his

11

own doorway. James Blair, a young attorney from Missouri, who was a brother of General Frank P. Blair, was visiting Governor Bent at the time, and he was also killed before the murderers left the house. Stephen Lee, who was acting as sheriff of the county, Pablo Armijo, prefect, and Cornelio Vigil, district attorney, were killed at about the same time, by different bands of the allied conspirators. The two men last named were both Mexicans, but they were loyal to the oaths which they had taken, to support the laws and government of the United States, and for this reason they were among the first victims of the massacre. Several other Americans were killed, whose names I do not now remember, and the savages then turned their attention to the women and children. I do not think there was a white woman of foreign birth living in the Mexican town at the time, nor is it probable that there were any full blood American children there. The half breed children were, however, marked for the slaughter, and as the Mexicans and Indians, all had dark complexions, the color of the hair and eyes was made the test of blood.

Spanish women who were married to Americans, had to disguise their children who had light hair and blue eyes, and some of those children still have a vivid recollection of having their faces and hair colored, to make them look as much as possible like the natives. Those who escaped in this way were the fortunate ones, and there were comparatively few of them. A majority of the half breeds were dispatched as summarily as Governor Bent and his friends had been. Among them, I recollect, was Narcisso Beaubien, a son of Judge Beaubien, who had lived among the Mexicans for years, and befriended both them and the Indians, in a thousand ways. Beaubien was a bright young fellow, who had just graduated from an eastern college, and proposed to make his home in the country, of which he was a native. His sympathies, however, were with the Americans, and he was not allowed to escape the fate of all those who were supposed to lean that way.

The bodies of some of those killed were horribly mutilated. All of the victims were scalped, and Governor Bent's head was cut off and carried about the town, to terrify women and children, and those Mexicans whom it was thought were not in full sympathy with the rebellion.

5. Lewis Garrard's Account

With Hatcher, I visited the house in which Governor Bent was murdered, who, with the district attorney, J. W. Liel, came from Santa Fé to issue a proclamation. While here in Fernández with his family, he was, one morning early, roused from sleep by the populace; who, with the aid of the Pueblos de Taos, were collected in front of his dwelling, striving to gain admittance. While they were effecting an entrance, he, with an ax, cut through an adobe wall into another house. The wife of the occupant, a clever though thriftless Canadian, heard him; and, with all her strength, rendered him assistance, though she was a Mexican. He retreated to a room, but seeing no way of escaping from the infuriated assailants, who fired upon him through a window, he spoke to his weeping wife and trembling children, clinging to him with all the tenacity of love and despair; and taking paper from his pocket, endeavored to write, but fast losing strength, he commended them to God and his brothers, and fell pierced by a Pueblo's ball. Rushing in and tearing off the gray-haired scalp, the Indians bore it away in triumph.

The district attorney, Liel, was scalped alive and dragged through the streets, his relentless persecutors pricking him with lances. After hours of acute suffering, he was thrown to one side in the inclement weather. He entreated, implored them earnestly to kill him—to end his misery. A compassionate Mexican at last closed the tragic scene by shooting him. Stephen Lee, brother to the General, was killed on his own housetop.

Narcisse Beaubien, son of the presiding judge of this district—the same young man in our company last fall—with his Indian slave, hid in an outhouse at the commencement of the massacre, under a straw-covered trough. The insurgents, on the search, thinking they had escaped, were leaving, but a woman—servant to the family—going to the housetop, called them, with the words—"Kill the young ones, and they will never be men to trouble us." They swarmed back and cruelly putting to death and scalping him and his slave, thus added two more to the unfortunate victims of unbounded passion and long-cherished revenge.

6. TERESINA BENT'S ACCOUNT OF HER FATHER'S DEATH

I was only five years old at the time, but I well remember every circumstance as if it was but yesterday. It was early in the morning and we were all in bed. We were awakened by the noise of many people, crowding into the placita. My father was at home from Santa Fé on a short visit and had refused a military escort. The night before he was warned of danger and urged to fly, but though there were several horses in the corrals, he declined. He had always treated everybody fairly and honestly and he felt that all were friends and he would not believe that they would turn against him. Hearing the noise he went to the door and tried to pacify the crowd yelling outside. In the adjoining room my mother, Mrs. Carson, and Mrs. Boggs, who were with us, and we children, were trembling with fear, all except my brother Alfredo. He was only ten years old, but had been reared on the frontier, and he took down the shotgun and going to my father's side said, 'Papa, let us fight them.'

While my father was parleying with the mob, Mrs. Carson and Mrs. Boggs, aided by an Indian woman who was a slave (*peon*), dug a hole through the adobe wall which separated our house from the next. They did it with only a poker and an old iron spoon; I have still the poker that they used. We children were first pushed through the hole and then the women crawled through after us. My mother kept calling to my father to come also, but for quite a while he would not. When he did try to escape he was already wounded and had been scalped alive. He crawled through the hole, holding his hand on the top of his bleeding head. But it was too late. Some of the men came after him through the hole and others came over the roof of the house and down into the yard. They broke down the doors and rushed upon my father. He was shot many times and fell dead at our feet. The pleading and tears of my mother and the sobbing of us children had no power to soften the hearts of the enraged Indians and Mexicans.

At first they were going to take the rest of us away as prisoners, but finally decided to leave us where we were. They ordered that no one should feed us, and then left us

14

alone with our great sorrow. We were without food and had no covering but our night-clothing, all that day and the next night. The body of our father remained on the floor in a pool of blood. We were naturally frightened, as we did not know how soon the miscreants might return to do us violence. At about three o'clock the next morning, some of our Mexican friends stole up to the house and gave us food and clothing. That day, also, they took my father to bury him. A few days later we were allowed to go to their house. Mrs. Carson and Mrs. Boggs were sheltered by a friendly old Mexican, who took them to his home, disguising them as squaws, and set them to grinding corn on metates in his kitchen.

7. George Ruxton's Account of the Fight at Turley's Mill

The morning after my arrival on Arkansa, two men, named Harwood and Markhead—the latter one of the most daring and successful trappers that ever followed this adventurous mountain-life, and whom I had intended to have hired as a guide to the valley of the Columbia the ensuing spring—started off to the settlement of New Mexico, with some packs of peltries, intending to bring back Taos whiskey (a very profitable article of trade amongst the mountain-men) and some bags of flour and Indian meal. I found on returning from my hunt that a man named John Albert had brought intelligence that the New Mexicans and Pueblo Indians had risen in the valley of Taos, and, as I have before mentioned, massacred Governor Bent and other Americans, and had also attacked and destroyed Turley's ranch on the Arroyo Hondo, killing himself and most of his men. Albert had escaped from the house, and, charging through the assailants, made for the mountains, and, traveling night and day and without food, had reached the Greenhorn with the news, and after recruiting for a couple of days had come on to the Arkansa with the intelligence, which threw the fierce mountaineers into a perfect frenzy. As Markhead and Harwood would have arrived in the settlements about the time of the rising, little doubt remained as to their fate, but it was not until nearly two

15

months after that any intelligence was brought concerning them. It seemed that they arrived at the Rio Colorado, the first New Mexican settlement, on the seventh or eighth day, when the people had just received news of the massacre in Taos. These savages, after stripping them of their goods, and securing, by treachery, their arms, made them mount their mules under the pretence of conducting them to Taos, there to be given up to the chief of the insurrection. They had hardly, however, left the village when a Mexican, riding behind Harwood, discharged his gun into his back: Harwood, calling to Markhead that he was "finished," fell dead to the ground. Markhead, seeing that his own fate was sealed, made no struggle, and was likewise shot in the back by several balls. They were then stripped and scalped and shockingly mutilated, and their bodies thrown into the bush by the side of the creek to be devoured by the wolves. They were both remarkably fine young men. Markhead was celebrated in the mountains for his courage and reckless daring, having had many almost miraculous escapes when in the very hands of hostile Indians. He had a few years ago accompanied Sir W. Drummond Stewart in one of his expeditions across the mountains. It happened that a half-breed of the company absconded one night with some animals belonging to Sir William, who, being annoyed at the circumstance, said hastily, and never dreaming that his offer would be taken up, that he would give five hundred dollars for the scalp of the thief. The next day Markhead rode into camp with the scalp of the unfortunate horse-thief hanging at the end of his rifle, and I believe received the reward, at least so he himself declared to me, for this act of mountain law. On one occasion, whilst trapping on the waters of the Yellow Stone, in the midst of the Blackfoot country, he came suddenly upon two or three lodges, from which the Indians happened to be absent. There was no doubt, from signs which he had previously discovered, that they were lying in wait for him somewhere on the stream to attack him when examining his traps, the Blackfeet, moreover, being most bitterly hostile to the white trappers, and killing them without mercy whenever an occasion offered. Notwithstanding the almost certainty that some of the Indians were close at hand, probably gone out for a supply of wood and would

16

very soon return, Markhead resolved to visit the lodges and help himself to anything worth taking that he might find there. The fire was burning, and meat was actually cooking in a pot over it. To this he did ample justice, emptying the pot in a very satisfactory manner, after which he tied all the blankets, dressed skins, mocassins, &c., into a bundle, and, mounting his horse, got safely off with his prize.

It was not always, however, that he escaped scathless, for his body was riddled with balls received in many a bloody affray with Blackfeet and other Indians.

Laforey, the old Canadian trapper, with whom I stayed at Red River, was accustomed of having possessed himself of the property found on the two mountaineers, and afterwards of having instigated the Mexicans to the barbarous murder. The hunters on Arkansa vowed vengeance against him, and swore to have his hair some day, as well as similar love-locks from the people of Red River. A war-expedition was also talked of to that settlement, to avenge the murder of their comrades, and ease the Mexicans of their mules and horses.

The massacre of Turley and his people, and the destruction of his mill, were not consummated without considerable loss to the barbarous and cowardly assailants. There were in the house, at the time of the attack, eight white men, including Americans, French Canadians, and one or two Englishmen, with plenty of arms and ammunition. Turley had been warned of the intended insurrection, but had treated the report with indifference and neglect, until one morning a man named Otterbees, in the employ of Turley, and who had been despatched to Santa Fé with several mule-loads of whiskey a few days before, made his appearance at the gate on horseback, and, hastily informing the inmates of the mill that the New Mexicans had risen and massacred Governor Bent and other Americans, galloped off. Even then Turley felt assured that he would not be molested, but, at the solicitations of his men, agreed to close the gate of the yard round which were the buildings of a mill and distillery, and make preparations for defence.

A few hours after a large crowd of Mexicans and Pueblo Indians made their appearance, all armed with guns and bows and arrows, and, advancing with a white flag, summoned Turley to surrender his house and the Americans in it, guaranteeing that his own life should be saved, but that every other American in the valley of Taos had to be destroyed; that the Governor and all the Americans at Fernandez and the rancho had been killed, and that not one was to be left alive in all New Mexico.

To this summons Turley answered that he would never surrender his house nor his men, and that, if they wanted it or them, "they must take them."

The enemy then drew off, and, after a short consultation, commenced the attack. The first day they numbered about five hundred, but the crowd was hourly augmented by the arrival of parties of Indians from the more distant pueblos, and of New Mexicans from Fernandez, La Cañada, and other places.

The building lay at the foot of a gradual slope in the sierra, which was covered with cedar-bushes. In front ran the stream of the Arroyo Hondo, about twenty yards from one side of the square, and on the other side was broken ground, which rose abruptly and formed the bank of the ravine. In rear, and behind the still-house, was some garden-ground enclosed by a small fence, and into which a small wicket-gate opened from the corral.

As soon as the attack was determined upon, the assailants broke, and, scattering, concealed themselves under the cover of the rocks and bushes which surrounded the house.

From these they kept up an incessant fire upon every exposed portion of the building where they saw the Americans preparing for defence.

They, on their parts, were not idle; not a man but was an old mountaineer, and each had his trusty rifle, with good store of ammunition. Wherever one of the assailants exposed a hand's-breadth of his person, there whistled a ball from an unerring barrel. The windows had been blockaded, loop-holes being left to fire through, and through these a lively fire was maintained. Already several of the enemy had bitten the dust, and parties were constantly seen bearing off the wounded up the banks of the Cañada. Darkness came on, and during the night a continual fire was kept up on the mill, whilst its defenders, reserving their ammunition, kept their posts with stern and silent determination. The night

18

was spent in running balls, cutting patches, and completing the defences of the building. In the morning the fight was renewed, and it was found that the Mexicans had effected a lodgment in a part of the stables, which were separated from the other portions of the building, and between which was an open space of a few feet. The assailants, during the night, had sought to break down the wall, and thus enter the main building, but the strength of the adobes and logs of which it was composed resisted effectually all their attempts.

Those in the stable seemed anxious to regain the outside, for their position was unavailable as a means of annoyance to the besieged, and several had darted across the narrow space which divided it from the other part of the building, and which slightly projected, and behind which they were out of the line of fire. As soon, however, as the attention of the defenders was called to this point, the first man who attempted to cross, and who happened to be a Pueblo chief, was dropped on the instant, and fell dead in the centre of the intervening space. It appeared an object to recover the body, for an Indian immediately dashed out to the fallen chief, and attempted to drag him within the cover of the wall. The rifle which covered the spot again poured forth its deadly contents, and the Indian springing into the air, fell over the body of his chief, struck to the heart. Another and another met with a similar fate, and at last three rushed at once to the spot, and, seizing the body by the legs and head, had already lifted it from the ground, when three puffs of smoke blew from the barricaded window, followed by the sharp cracks of as many rifles, and the three daring Indians added their number to the pile of corpses which now covered the body of the dead chief.

As yet the besieged had met with no casualties; but after the fall of the seven Indians, in the manner above described, the whole body of assailants, with a shout of rage, poured in a rattling volley, and two of the defenders of the mill fell mortally wounded. One, shot through the loins, suffered great agony, and was removed to the still-house, where he was laid upon a large pile of grain, as being the softest bed to be found.

In the middle of the day the assailants renewed the attack more fiercely than before, their baffled attempts adding to

19

their furious rage. The little garrison bravely stood to the defence of the mill, never throwing away a shot, but firing coolly, and only when a fair mark was presented to their unerring aim. Their ammunition, however, was fast failing, and, to add to the danger of their situation, the enemy set fire to the mill, which blazed fiercely, and threatened destruction to the whole building. Twice they succeeded in overcoming the flames, and, taking advantage of their being thus occupied, the Mexicans and Indians charged into the corral, which was full of hogs and sheep, and vented their cowardly rage upon the animals, spearing and shooting all that came in their way. No sooner, however, were the flames extinguished in one place, than they broke out more fiercely in another; and as a successful defence was perfectly hopeless, and the numbers of the assailants increased every moment, a council of war was held by the survivors of the little garrison, when it was determined, as soon as night approached, that every one should attempt to escape as best he might, and in the mean time the defence of the mill was to be continued.

Just at dusk, Albert and another man ran to the wicket-gate which opened into a kind of enclosed space, and in which was a number of armed Mexicans. They both rushed out at the same moment, discharging their rifles full in the faces of the crowd. Albert, in the confusion, threw himself under the fence, whence he saw his companion shot down immediately, and heard his cries for mercy, mingled with shrieks of pain and anguish, as the cowards pierced him with knives and lances. Lying without motion under the fence, as soon as it was quite dark he crept over the logs and ran up the mountain, travelled day and night, and, scarcely stopping or resting, reached the Greenhorn, almost dead with hunger and fatigue. Turley himself succeeded in escaping from the mill and in reaching the mountain unseen. Here he met a Mexican, mounted on a horse, who had been a most intimate friend of the unfortunate man for many years. To this man Turley offered his watch (which was treble its worth) for the use of his horse, but was refused. The inhuman wretch, however, affected pity and commiseration for the fugitive, and advised him to go to a certain place, where he would bring or send him assistance; but on reaching the mill, which was now a mass of fire, he immediately informed the Mexicans of his place of concealment, whither a large party instantly proceeded and shot him to death. Two others escaped and reached Santa Fé in safety. The mill and Turley's house were sacked and gutted, and all his hard-earned savings, which were considerable, and concealed in gold about the house, were discovered, and of course seized upon, by the victorious Mexicans.

The Indians, however, met a few days after with a severe retribution. The troops marched out of Santa Fé, attacked their pueblo, and levelled it to the ground, killing many hundreds of its defenders, and taking many prisoners, most of whom were hanged.

Jim Beckwourth
(Beckwourth, 1856)

III. The News Spreads

On my arrival at Santa Fé I found affairs in a very disturbed state. Colonel Doniphan had just gained the battle of Brasito, and was carrying all before him in that section of the country. He had forwarded orders to Santa Fé for a field battery, in order to make a demonstration against Chihuahua. Major Clarke was intrusted with the duty of conveying the artillery to the colonel. Scarcely had he departed when we received intelligence of an insurrection in Taos. The information was first communicated by an Indian from a village between Santa Fé and Taos, who reported to General Price that the Mexicans had massacred all the white inhabitants of that place, and that a similar massacre was contemplated in Santa Fé, of which report full information could be obtained by the arrest of a Mexican who was then conveying a letter from the priest in Taos to the priest in Santa Fé. A watch was immediately set upon the priest's house, and a Mexican was seen to enter. The guard approached the door to arrest the man as he issued, but he, being apprised of the action of the authorities, left the house by another door and escaped.

At night their came a violent rapping at my gate, and on going to open it I perceived my friend, Charles Towne, who, on being admitted, clasped me around the neck, and gave vent to uncontrolled emotion. Perceiving that something alarming had occurred, I invited him into the house, spread refreshments before him and allowed him time to recover himself. He then informed me that he had escaped almost by a miracle from Taos, where all the American residents had been killed. He was a resident there, having married a girl of New Mexico, and his wife's father had apprised him that he had better effect his escape, if possible, for if he was caught he would be inevitably massacred. His father-in-law provided him with a good horse, and he retreated into the woods, where, after considerable risk and anxiety, he providentially eluded the assassins.

On receiving this alarming information, I lost no time in repairing to the headquarters of General Price, accompanied by my informant, who related the above particulars. General Price immediately adopted the most effective measures. He assembled his officers, and instructed them to set a close watch upon the house of every Mexican in the city, and to suffer no person to pass in or out; he also ordered that every American should hold himself in readiness for service during the night. Before morning several of the most influential Mexican citizens were placed under arrest. In searching them, important conspiracies were brought to light. Correspondence, implicating the most considerable residents, was read, and a plot was detected of subjecting Santa Fé to the same St. Bartholomew massacre as had just been visited upon Taos. The city was placed under martial law, and every American that could shoulder a musket was called into immediate service. All the ox-drivers, mule-drivers, merchants, clerks, and commissariat-men were formed into rank and file, and placed in a condition for holding the city.

9. Dick Wootton at Pueblo

When they had made an end of the massacre at Taos, these bloody butchers proceeded to Arroyo Honda, twelve miles from Taos, where there was another American settlement, and killed everybody they could find there.

Two men made their escape from that place, and one of them started for Santa Fe and the other for Pueblo, to carry the news of the slaughter to those places. The distance from Taos to Pueblo was about one hundred and sixty-five miles. Pueblo was not a town at that time, you understand. What we called "the Pueblo," stood on the site of the present town. It was an adobe fort, built by the trappers, which had become headquarters for a considerable number of the mountain men, and was something of a trading post. I was there at the time of the Taos massacre, and about five days later John Albert, who had managed some way or other to make his escape from Arroyo Honda, came into the Pueblo, bringing the news of the Mexican uprising and its bloody sequel. He had traveled the whole distance on foot, and was almost exhausted when he reached us.

When Albert had laid before us all the details of the tragedy, our little band of trappers held a council of war, to determine what we should do. The situation was as perplexing as it was distressing. The friendships of the mountain men were warm friendships. We had never seen the time when we were not ready to attempt the rescue of a friend whose life was in danger, and it was seldom indeed that the killing or wounding of one of our number had gone unavenged.

Among those who had been so brutally murdered at Taos and Arroyo Honda, were men who had been my warmest and best friends, ever since I came to the country, and I felt that I should, if possible, do something toward securing punishment of their murderers, and protecting the property which they had left, for the use of those who were entitled to it. What to do, however, was the question. We should not have hesitated much about attacking an ordinary band of roving Indians, but to undertake to put down what seemed to be a formidable rebellion, was of course out of our line. We did not know what might be going on at Santa Fe, or how long it would be, before we could expect any help from the·government forces, and without such assistance, the small party of volunteers that we should have been able to muster, could have accomplished nothing.

We parleyed over the matter awhile, and reached the conclusion that there were soldiers enough at Santa Fe to put down the rebellion and having agreed upon this point we reached the further conclusion, that it was our duty to render them all the assistance possible.

This determined our action, and five of us mounted our horses and started across the country toward Taos. It took us several days to make the trip, and we approached the place very carefully. We made our way into the high mountains

Dick Wootton
(Conard, *Uncle Dick Wootton*, 1891)

east of Taos, and from there we could look down on the town, and see pretty well what was going on, without being discovered ourselves. As we could discover no sign of the arrival of the soldiers, we knew that it was not safe for us to venture further.

In the meantime, Thomas Tobin, the messenger who had left Arroyo Honda, with the news of the massacre at that place and at Taos, had reached Santa Fe, and Colonel Price had lost no time in marching against the rebels. He met the first force of Mexicans and Indians at La Cañada, some distance out on the Taos road from Santa Fe, and soon had them on the run. He then sent Captain Burgwin, with two companies of troops, on toward Taos. Colonel Ceran St. Vrain, Governor Bent's partner, accompanied Captain Burgwin, with about sixty volunteers, picked up in Santa Fe. At Embudo they had another skirmish with the insurgents, and did not reach Taos until the third of February.

We were watching for them, and saw them when they marched into the town. The hostiles had all gathered at the Pueblo de Taos, and fortified themselves in and about the old church. The soldiers marched to the Pueblo and fired a few shots, but as night was coming on, they returned to Fernandez de Taos, and went into camp for the night.

10. LEWIS GARRARD ON THE ARKANSAS

On the morning of the 28th, Smith and I were in the log house, trading *o-ne-a-wokst* (beads) to an old squaw for *o-ne-a-voke* (a piece of meat). While asking for an addition to our already large contribution, she pointed with her mouth to an approaching object, saying, "*Po-ome! num-whit veheo*" (Blackfoot! look yonder, there's a white man").

Coming close, he hailed us, "How are ye, John?"

"What! Louy, old coon, down hyar? How's times to Fort William!—but let's see, you's the one as run 'meat' for them gover'ment fellers to Bent's ranch—eh?"

"Yes! an' this child was mighty nigh losin' his har, *he* was."

"How?"

"Them darned Spaniards!"

27

"H——! anybody 'gone under' to Touse?"

"Yes! Guvner Charles."

"Wa-agh! but them palous'll pay for their scalpin' yet, I'm thinkin'."

We went in the lodge, where the men, after recovering from the surprise of seeing an old *compañero*, were told the sad news of Governor Bent's death, and while Louy was stowing away huge pieces of buffalo, he was interrogated by the anxious traders—

"Louy, tell all 'bout the whole consarn; it's all over now, an' can't be worse. I'spect the niggurs got my woman too," said Fisher, who was a resident of Taos, the scene of the massacre, "Who else is under, 'sides Charles?"

"*Well*, you see the Purblos [Pueblas de Taos] was mity mad fur the 'Mericans to come in thar diggins an' take everything so easy like; an', as Injun blood *is* bad an' sneakin', they swore to count coups when they could. So when Charles was down to Touse to see his woman, the palous charged afore sunrise. The portal was too strong fur 'em, an' they broke in with axes, an' a Purblo, cached behint a pile of dobies, shot him with a Nor-west fusee twice, an' skulped him."

"Scalped *him*—scalped Charles?" cried the men, partly swinging to their feet and clutching their knives, "Thar be heap of wolf meat afore long—sartain!"

"Yes! an' they took the trail for Santy Fee; but afore they left, Stephe Lee dropped in *his* tracks too. 'Hell!' says I, the palou as threw that arrer is marked,' an' so he is—Wa'agh!"

"Was Narcisse Beaubien killed, Louy?" asked I.

"Who? that young feller as kem with the wagons, last fall, with St. Vrain?"

"Yes, the same."

"Oh! he's gone beaver 'long with the rest. He was Mexican blood, an' so much the better fur them. They had a big dance when his topknot was off. Well, you see," commencing once more, "a band of the devils got to the Pionel ranch, over Touse Mountain, and back agin with the biggest kind of cavyard. Maybe *coups* wasn't counted that trip. the sojers—a lot of greenhorns and Dutchmen—came to Purgatoire, this side of Raton. Frank De Lisle had the company's wagons, an' the boys thar. We cached along the train fur the Arkansa—*well* we did! Mule meat went a wolfin' that spree—Wagh!"

"Where is Drinker? He was at the ranch, I believe."

"Out in the pinyon, that morning, with his big Saint Loui' gun—a Jake Hawkins gun, *she* was, eh? He had bullets an inch long, with a sharp piint—be doggoned ef they wasn't some, eh?—We had to leave him, but I guess he'll come in safe."

"Will they take Santy Fee, think ye, Louy?" inquired Fisher.

"Now that's more than this hos kin tell. He hasn't made 'medicine' yet; but I'm afraid the 'Mericans *will* 'go under.' "

Louy was called from the lodge by William Bent. We pitied William. His murdered brother, being much older than himself and George, was loved and respected as a father.

The news had quite a depressing effect upon us. We were even apprehensive of our own safety in case the Santa Féan forces were overpowered; for it was probable the country, from El Paso to El Valle de Taos, had revolted; and, as Bent's Fort contained much of value and was an important post, a Mexican expedition might well be expected.

When the Indians learned the death of their old friend, *Wohpi ve-heo*—'the gray-haired white man"—criers were sent out, and the people harangued. After consultation, the chiefs proposed that the young men should march to Taos and scalp every Mexican within reach. But Mr. Bent, thanking them, declined, saying that the soldiers at the fort would go if necessary.

At the following dawn, Mr. Bent and I left for the fort, some forty miles distant, taking no baggage but the robes strapped to the saddles.

The morning was cold and cloudy, in consonance with our moody taciturnity. Keeping the south bank of the river for some miles, we attempted a ford. Our fractious mules gave much trouble, detaining us a vexatious half-hour; we then broke the ice, and dragged and pushed in their unwilling feet by main strength.

While breasting the strong wind, which keeps the trail nicely swept as with a broom, we saw, emerging from a patch of high marsh-grass, skirting the belt of cottonwoods on the river's margin, a Mexican, mounted on a strong, iron-gray horse. He wore, in lieu of a hat, a handkerchief bound over his head, under the edges of which long jetty locks flitted to the breeze. His right hand grasped a short bow and a few arrows. He was passing at a gallop, when Bent, with his cocked rifle, shouted in Spanish to stop. The man stated that he belonged to William Tharpe's company; but the skulk's restless eye and his every motion seemed to indicate more than he told. After a searching cross-examination, Bent told him to *"vamos, prento!"* ("go quick"), or he would send a ball through him, anyhow. I expected to see the Mexican pitch from his horse through the aid of a bullet. Bent turned to follow him, expressing a regret at not having taken a shot.

By sundown we reached the fort, having traveled the entire day without ten minutes' halt, or scarcely a word of conversation. Fifty dirty, uncouth, green-looking Missourians, in command of Captain Jackson, hung about us as we left the saddles.

There was much excitement in regard to the massacre, some expecting a Mexican army to appear on the hill across the river; others, strutting inside the high and secure fort walls, gasconaded and looked fierce enough to stare a mad "buffler" out of countenance, declaring themselves ready to wade up to their necks in Mexican blood. Everyone, however, had cause for fear, as the American force was known to be small and much weakened by being scattered in small herding parties throughout the province. The traders, etc., proposed to push right on to Taos: steal all the animals, "raise" all the attainable Mexican "hair," burn every ranch and "charge" generally.

A while before dusk, an express from the Arkansas Pueblo, seventy miles above, arrived with the news that the United States detachment of volunteers stationed there were awaiting orders from Jackson, the superior in command. But the Captain (Jackson) would not act without orders from Colonel Price, at Santa Fé, at that time likely a prisoner. So the idea of aid in that quarter was reluctantly abandoned.

Louy Simonds, on leaving the ranch, cut across the

country, by that means preceding the wagons several days. The morning after our arrival, Frank De Lisle's wagons corralled in front of the fort. My old friends, the Canadian teamsters, shook my hand heartily—finer fellows were never soaked by the prairie storms.

About ten o'clock, as I was standing at the far end of the court, a tall man stalked in the gate, looking wildly around. A long-browned rifle rested on his shoulder, with that exquisite *negligé* air—firm yet careless-appearing—his long, black, uncombed hair hung in strings from beneath his greasy wool hat; and a frowning moustache gave a Satanic cast to his features. On his feet were thick moccasins, and to judge from the cut, of his own fashioning. His pantaloons, of gray cassinet, were threadbare and rudely patched with buckskin. Instead of a coat, a blanket was thrown over the shoulder and fastened, at the waist, by a black leather belt, in which was thrust a brass-studded leather sheath, sustaining a "Green River" of no small pretensions as to length; and which, had it the power of speech, might dwell with ecstatic pleasure on the praise of choice morceaus of "fleece" severed by its keen edge—perchance astonish with the recital of the number of "Yutes," whose "hump ribs" have been savagely tickled with its searching point. His quick eye, wandering, alighted on me, followed by—

"How are you?"

"Why, Drinker!" exclaimed I, in the utmost surprise, and taking his outstretched hand, "I'm glad to see you—Louy Simonds told us that the Spaniards had taken your 'hair.' "

"Oh p'shaw! not yet, I can assure you."

"Did you travel by yourself all the way?"

"No, not quite. I went out hunting that morning, and became so interested in a beaver dam that it was night before the ranch was reached again. Our men were gone, but I cooked some of the "goat" I had that day killed, and on Louy's old deerskins, lying about camp, I slept until morning. I then followed their trail, on foot, toward the Vermaho. The second day I caught up to a train, but they being too slow, I pushed ahead by myself. I overtook the company's wagons yesterday, and have been alone the rest of the time."

"That's a quick trip for a pedestrian. How long were you in coming? It's about 170 miles."

"Oh! a little over six days. My moccasins nearly gone the way of all flesh"—replied he, looking at his feet.

Mr. Bent determining that something should be done, called his men together; and, stating the facts of the case, ended by saying they could go or stay—as they choosed. Every one offered his services.

It was in the afternoon of the next day that the party was started, consisting of twenty-three men. Bransford was in charge of the seventeen employees and the wagon; the other five were free. One was Lucien Maxwell, a hunter to Frémont's expedition in 1842, a resident of the valley of Taos, and a son-in-law to Judge Beaubien (Narcisse's father). Manuel Le Févre—Lajeunesse and Tom—claimed a local habitation in Taos. They, very fortunately for themselves, happened to be on the opposite side of the mountain at the time of the massacre.

We crossed the river into Nueve Méjico at the fort ford, and followed the Santa Fé Trail, which kept the river bank. Five of us were mounted; the rest were to get animals at the Purgatoire, ninety miles distant. The object of the expedition in which we were about to engage was to travel as far as we could toward Taos; kill and scalp every Mexican to be found, and collect all the animals belonging to the Company and the United States.

The wind rose at dark, driving the most of us down by the water's edge; where, sheltered by the high banks, we talked and smoked. The Canadians were above us, chattering in their usual glib style, when a sound like distant thunder filled the air. Down they rushed, all talking at once. We knew that it could not be thunder at this time of year, and the conclusion at which we soon arrived was that a battle was taking place in Taos. Although it is a long distance there by the road and a lofty mountain intervenes, it is not more than thirty-five or forty miles in a direct line. It was a hazardous trip for us to venture so far in the Mexican territory, with no knowledge of affairs at Santa Fé and elsewhere except those of an alarming nature; and we knew too well the carelessness and paucity of the American soldiery. We felt the Mexicans to be an injured people, possessed of vindictive tempers, who would, with a prospect of success and under the guidance of brave leaders, revolt and fight well.

We were apprehensive that a Mexican force had overpowered the Americans at the Purgatoire (a day's ride in advance), and was on its way to Bent's Fort. Our position was anything but enviable. Maxwell, Le Févre, Lajeunesse, and Tom were cast down with thought of their families, who might, at that moment, be subject to the lawlessness of the infuriated populace. It was a gloomy night to those who, in anxious wakefulness, passed the long dark hours till morning.

An American Camp Scene
(Richardson, *Journal*, 1848)

IV. Action at Mora

11. U.S. GOVERNMENT PROCLAMATION

On the 25th ultimo Captain Hendly (of Colonel Willock's battalion), who was in command of the grazing parties on the Rio Moro, marched with 80 men to the town of Moro to suppress the insurrection there and arrest the murderers of Messrs. Culver, Waldo, Noyes, and others, who were massacred at that place.

He found a body of Mexicans under arms prepared to defend the town, and while forming his men into line for attack, a small party of the insurgents were seen running from the hills. A detachment was ordered to cut them off, which was attacked by the main body of the enemy. A general engagement immediately ensued, the Mexicans retreating to the town and firing from the windows and loopholes in their houses. Captain Hendly and his men closely pursued, rushing into their houses with them, shooting some, and running others through with bayonets.

A large body of the insurgents had taken possession of an old fort and commenced a fire from the loopholes upon the Americans. Captain H., with a small party, had taken possession of an apartment in the fort, and, while preparing to fire it, was shot by a ball from an adjoining room. He fell, and died in a few minutes. Our men, having no artillery and the fort being impregnable without it, retired to Las Vegas. The enemy had 25 killed and 17 taken prisoners. Our loss, 1 killed and 2 or 3 wounded.

On the 1st instant, Captain Morin, who had been ordered from Santa Fe by Colonel Willock to succeed Captain Hendly in the command, proceeded with a body of men and one piece of cannon to Moro and razed the towns (Upper and Lower Moro) to the ground, the insurgents having fled to the mountains. Several Mexicans were captured, supposed to be concerned in the murder of Messrs. Culver, Waldo, and others, and after many threats were forced to show where the bodies were buried. Seven of them were found and carried to Las Vegas for interment.— Government Printing Office, Santa Fe, February 15, 1847.

12. I. R. HENDLEY TO STERLING PRICE

HEADQUARTERS GRAZING DETACHMENT,
Las Vegas, January 23, 1847.

SIR:

Below is an account of the circumstances that have lately transpired in this region.

On the evening of the 20th instant myself and Lieut. N. J. Williams happened at this place just as the town had assembled in general council to hear the same circular read that has (been) forwarded to you from Taos. The alcalde of this (place) declared against the insurrection, and stopped the express and forwarded the letter to you. Early the next day I took possession of this place with part of my command and have ordered the balance to join me to-day. Lieutenant McKamey has also joined me with his forces. I have ordered the different grazing parties to rendezvous their stock about 7 miles below this place and the men to report themselves here ready for service as quick as possible.

News reached this place this morning that Messrs. Waldo, Culver, and two other Americans had been killed in Mora and that a United States grazing party had been cut to pieces night before last. Yesterday morning I started Lieutenant Hawkins, with 35 men, to find out what had become of some trains that I heard were on this side of the mountains, with orders to bring them in, if possible, as I consider it of great importance that they should be brought in safe.

My movements so far have been in anticipation of your orders, and have (been) such as to place the whole force in this section for offensive and defensive operation. I ordered Lieutenant McKamey to bring up the balance of his forces and some grazers that are near him to this place. To-morrow

36

I expect to go against Mora with part of my force, where it is reported that the Mexicans are embodied. Our ammunition is very short, there only being about 10 rounds of cartridges and 25 pounds each powder and lead that I yesterday got from a Mr. Kid. It is of great importance that I should be quickly supplied.

If you will forward me one or two pieces of artillery, well manned, and plenty of ammunition, I pledge myself to subdue and keep in check every town this side of the mountains. Every town and village except this (I did not give it time) and Tucoloti have declared in favor of the insurrection. The whole population appear ripe for the insurrection. I will try and keep you apprised of all movements in this quarter. It is said that a large force, probably 1,000 men, are marching from Taos toward Santa Fe, Toma, Ortes, and Archuletta at their head. The Mora men—I do not know what leaders they have, but hope to be better able to tell you in a few days.

I am collecting all the provisions I can at this point, for I think you will find that troops must be kept here, as it would keep San Miguel, Mora, and surrounding country in check.

If you conclude to forward me the artillery, send me word and I will meet it. I want permission to purchase corn to feed from 70 to 100 horses, as some mounted men will be required for two or three weeks. My force by to-morrow or next day will amount, including grazing parties and other Americans that have joined me for protection, to about 225 men, say 175 efficient men, out of which Lieutenant Hawkins is now absent with 35 men.

Hoping that you may approve of what I have already done and send me full instruction and plenty of ammunition,

I remain your obedient servant,

I. R. HENDLEY,
Captain Company G., Commanding at Vegas.
Col. S. PRICE.

P.S.—The express sent by Lieutenant-Colonel Willock was attacked at the San Bernal Spring, and only escaped by deserting their mules and taking to the mountains afoot. The action against the population here I would suggest should be active and vigorous.

I. R. H.

13. I. R. HENDLEY TO STERLING PRICE

JANUARY 23, 1847—2 o'clock p.m.

SIR:

An express has just arrived from Lieutenant Hawkins, at the Mora River, that he had met Captain Murphy, escorted by a detachment of Captain Jackson's company. Lieutenant Hawkins will escort Captain Murphy from Mora to this place, and from here I will go with him myself until I meet an escort from Santa Fe, which I desire you will hurry on as fast as possible, and let them bring me the artillery if you conclude to send me any. Captain Jackson's men will return from the Mora to meet the trains, which are one day's march from that place. No fresh news about the Mexicans except Lieutenant Hawkins's report that a parcel of the Apache Indians have joined with the Mexicans. So Mr. Wells at the Mora has heard. The escorting of Captain Murphy will much impede my operations here.

Respectfully,

I. R. HENDLEY, *Captain, etc.*

Colonel PRICE.

14. T. C. MCKAMEY TO STERLING PRICE

BAGAS (VEGAS), *January 25, 1847.*

SIR:

The grazing parties of this part of the country have all assembled at Begos and we are about 250 strong. We learned a few days since that there were a force of Mexicans assembled at Mora town, and on yesterday we started up to that place with a force of 80 men under the command of Captain Hendley for the purpose of ascertaining their strength, and on our arrival we found that there were 150 or 200 men. We halted in the suburbs of the town and were consulting whether we would attack the town or not; and while we were consulting there 4 Mexicans came running down out of the mountains; 6 of us mounted our horses and aimed to cut them off from the town, but the Mexicans came running out to their relief and at that time Captain Hendley ordered the company to mount and charge on them; and they fired on us two or three times and then retreated to their fort, and we cut off 15 and took them prisoners.

We kept up a firing for a considerable length of time. After killing from 15 to 20 we commenced burning and tearing down their houses, and had succeeded in getting into one end of the fort—Captain Hendley, myself, and about 10 men—and fired on them ten or twelve times, when Captain Hendley received a shot and died immediately. We took him out of the room and carried him some 200 yards. It was then growing late, and being informed that there were from three to five hundred troops started from that place on this morning for Santa Fe, and fearing that they might be called back, we retreated with our men and prisoners to Begos where we are well fortified, where we arrived with 3 men slightly wounded. If we had one or two pieces of artillery to scare them out of their dens we could whip all the Mexicans this side of the ridge.

Yours, in haste,

T. C. McKamey, *Lieutenant.*

Colonel Price.

15. W. S. Murphy to Sterling Price

Vegas. *January 25, 1847.*

I enclose to you Lieutenant McKamey's report of the battle of Mora town, which commenced this morning and lasted about three hours. I arrived here in the evening of the 23rd and did not think it prudent to leave until the command returned from Mora town, which has just returned bringing the dead body of Captain Hendley, the only loss on our side. The loss on the part of Mexicans, so far as ascertained, is 15 killed and 15 prisoners, with whom I will commence my march on the 27th, and expect to arrive in Santa Fe on 30th instant. There is but one provision train on this side of the Raton Mountains. It will encamp at the crossing of the Mora to-morrow night. Mr. Campbell has gone with 15 men to procure fresh cattle to assist it to this place.

I have taken the responsibility to send Lieutenant Oxley, Company O, Second Regiment, in command of 18 men, from Mora back to protect the train, which I hope will prove satisfactory. Companies M and N grazing camps have been robbed of all their animals except five or six; no men killed. The animals at Bent farm have all been taken. Seven men killed at this camp; report says all volunteers, some of them belonging to Captain Jackson's company. The bearer of this will inform you of particulars not prudent to commit to writing.

Yours, respectfully,

W. S. MURPHY,
Captain Infantry Missouri Volunteers.

P.S.—Romulus Culver, of Chariton; Ludlow Waldo, of Jackson; Mr. Prewit, of Santa Fe; Lewis Cabano, of Missouri, and four or five in company were taken prisoners, robbed, and shot at Mora town on or about the 20th of the month. The leader of the forces at that place is by the name of Cortez.

V. Price's Advance

16. Proclamation by Provisional Governor Donaciano Vigil

The provisional governor of the Territory to its inhabitants:

Fellow Citizens:

Your regularly appointed governor had occasion to go on private business as far as the town of Taos. A popular insurrection, headed by Pablo Montoya and Manuel Cortez, who raised the cry of revolution, resulted in the barbarous assassination of his excellency, the governor, of the greater part of the Government officials, and some private citizens. Pablo Montoya, whom you already know, notorious for his insubordination and restlessness, headed a similar insurrection in September, 1837. Destitute of any sense of shame, he brought his followers to this capital, entered into an arrangement, deserted, as a reward for their fidelity, the unfortunate Montoyas, Esquibal, and Chopon, whose fate you know, and retired himself, well paid for his exploits, to his den at Taos. The whole population left the weight of their execration fall on others, and this brigand they left living on his wits—for he has no home or known property, and is engaged in no occupation. Of what kind of people is his gang composed? Of the insurgent Indian population of Taos, and of others as abandoned and desperate as their rebellious chief. Discreet and respectable men are anxiously awaiting the forces of the Government in order to be relieved from the anarchy in which disorder has placed them, and this relief will speedily be afforded them. In the year 1837 this mischievous fool took, as a motto for his perversity, the word "canton," and now it is "the reunion of Taos!" Behold the works of the champion who guides the revolution! And can there be a single man of sense who would voluntarily join his ranks? I should think not.

Another of his pretended objects is to wage war against the foreign government. Why, if he is so full of patriotism, did he not exert himself and lead troops to prevent the entry of American forces in the month of August, instead of glutting his insane passions and showing his martial valor by the brutal sacrifice of defenseless victims, and this at the very time when an arrangement between the two Governments, with regard to boundaries, was expected? Whether this country has to belong to the Government of the United States or return to its native Mexico, is it not a gross absurdity to foment rancorous feelings toward people with whom we are either to compose one family, or to continue our commercial relations? Unquestionably it is.

To-day or to-morrow a respectable body of troops will commence their march for the purpose of quelling the disorders of Pablo Montoya, in Taos. The Government is determined to pursue energetic measures toward all the refractory until they are reduced to order, as well as to take care of and protect honest and discreet men; and I pray you that, hearkening to the voice of reason, for the sake of the common happiness and your own preservation, you will keep yourselves quiet and engaged in your private affairs.

The term of my administration is purely transitory. Neither my qualifications nor the ad interim character, according to the organic law in which I take the reins of government, encourage me to continue in so difficult and thorny a post, the duties of which are intended for individuals of greater enterprise and talents; but I protest to you, in the utmost fervor of my heart, that I will devote myself exclusively to endeavoring to secure you all the prosperity so much desired by your fellow citizen and friend,

DONACIANO VIGIL.

SANTA FE, *January 22, 1847.*

17. PROCLAMATION BY DONACIANO VIGIL

The provisional governor of the Territory to its inhabitants:

The gang of Pablo Montoya and Cortez, in Taos, infatuated in consequence of having sacrificed to their caprice his excellency, the governor, and other peaceable citizens, and commenced their great work of plunder by sacking the houses of their victims, according to principles proclaimed by them, for the purpose of making proselytes, yesterday encountered in the vicinity of La Cañada the forces of the Government restorative of order and peace, and in that place, unfortunately for them, their triumph ended; for they were routed with the loss of many killed and 44 prisoners, upon whom the judgment of the law will fall.

Their hosts were composed of scoundrels and desperadoes, so that it may be said that the war was one of the rabble against honest and discreet men; not one of the latter has as yet been found among this crew of vagabonds, unless, perhaps, some one actuated by the fear of losing his life while in their power or of being robbed of his property. The Government has the information, and congratulates itself that within ten days the inquietude caused you by the cry of alarm raised in Taos will cease, and peace, the precursor of the felicity of the country, will return to take her seat on the altar of concord and reciprocal confidence.

The ringleaders of the conspiracy, if they should be apprehended, will receive the reward due to their signal crimes, and the Government, which for the present has been compelled to act with energy in order to crush the head of the revolutionary hydra which began to show itself in Taos, will afterwards adopt lenient meaures, in order to consolidate the union of all the inhabitants of this beautiful country under the aegis of law and reason.

I hope, therefore, that, your minds being now relieved of past fears, you will think only on the security and protection of the law; and, uniting with your Government, will afford it the aid of your intelligence, in order that it may secure to you the prosperity desired by your fellow-citizen and friend,

DONACIANO VIGIL.

SANTA FE, *January 25, 1847.*

18. U.S. GOVERNMENT CICRULAR—Santa Fe, 15 Feb. 1847

On the morning of the 20th of January intelligence of the massacre of Governor Bent was brought to Santa Fe by an

Indian runner. A circular letter was also received by the priest at this place, stating that the Mexicans and Indians of Taos had risen against the invaders of their country, and requesting him to join them. This letter was handed to Colonel Price by the priest. Various reports reached this place of the advance of the enemy and their near approach. In consequence of these reports Colonel Price determined to march out of Santa Fe and meet them in the open field. He took with him 340 men, composed of Captain Angney's battalion of infantry, portions of six companies of the Second Regiment, and a company of citizens and mountaineers under the command of Captain St. Vrain, leaving Lieutenant-Colonel Willock in command of this post with a force composed of his own battalion, three companies of the Second Regiment, a portion of Captain Fischer's company of light artillery, and one company of regulars. On the evening of the 24th Colonel Price encountered the enemy at Cañada, numbering about 2,000 men, under the command of Gens. Jesus Tafoya, Pablo Chavez, and Pablo Montoya. The enemy were posted on the hills commanding each side of the road. About 2 o'clock p.m. a brisk fire from the artillery, under the command of Lieutenants Dyer (of the Regular Army) and Harsentiver, was opened upon them, but from their being so much scattered, it had but little effect.

The artillery were within such short distance as to be exposed to a hot fire, which either wounded or penetrated the clothes of 19 out of the 20 men who served the guns. Colonel Price, seeing the slight effect which the artillery had upon them, ordered Captain Angney with his battalion to charge the hill, which was gallantly done, being supported by Captain St. Vrain, of the citizens, and Lieutenant White, of the Carrol companies. The charge routed them and a scattering fight ensued, which lasted until sundown. Our loss was 2 killed and 7 wounded. The Mexicans acknowledged a loss of 36 killed and 45 taken prisoners. The enemy retreated toward Taos, their stronghold. Colonel Price, on the 27th, took up his line of march for Taos, and again encountered them at El Emboda on the 29th. They were discovered in the thick brush on each side of the road at the entrance of a defile by a party of spies, who immediately fired upon them. Captain Burgwin, who had that morning joined Colonel Price with his company of dragoons, hearing the firing, came up, together with Captain St. Vrain's and Lieutenant White's companies. A charge was made by the three companies, resulting in the total rout of the Mexicans and Indians. The battle lasted about half an hour, but the pursuit was kept up for two hours.

The march was resumed on the next day and met with no opposition until the evening of the 3d of February, at which time they arrived at the Pueblo de Taos, where they found the Mexicans and Indians strongly fortified. A few rounds were fired by the artillery that evening, but it was deemed advisable not to make a general attack then but wait until morning. The attack was commenced in the morning by two batteries under the command of Lieutenants Dyer and Wilson of the Regular Army, and Lieutenant Harsentiver of the light artillery, by throwing shells into the town. About 12 o'clock a. m. a charge was ordered and gallantly executed by Captain Burgwin's company, supported by Captain McMillan's company and Captain Angney's battalion of infantry, supported by Captain Barbee's company. The church which had been used as a part of the fortifications was taken by this charge. The fight was hotly contested until night, when two white flags were hoisted, but were immediately shot down. In the morning the fort was surrendered. In this battle fell Captain Burgwin, than whom a braver soldier or better man never poured out his blood in his country's cause.

The total loss of the Mexicans in the three engagements is estimated at 282 killed; the number of their wounded is unknown. Our total loss was 11 killed and 47 wounded, 3 of whom have since died.

19. FROM REPORT BY COLONEL STERLING PRICE TO THE ADJUTANT GENERAL—*15 February 1847*

News of these events reached me on the 20th of January; and letters from the rebels calling upon the inhabitants of the Rio Abajo for aid, were intercepted. It was now ascertained that the enemy was approaching this city, and that their force was continually being increased by the inhabitants of the towns along their line of march.

In order to prevent the enemy from receiving any further reinforcements in that manner, I determined to meet them as soon as possible. Supposing that the detachment of the necessary troops would weaken the garrison of Santa Fe too much, I immediately ordered up from Albuquerque Major Edmonson, 2d regiment Missouri mounted volunteers, and Captain Burgwin, with their respective commands, directing Captain Burgwin to leave one company of dragoons at this post, and to join me with the other. Major Edmonson was directed to remain in Santa Fe.

Captain Giddings, company A, 2d regiment Missouri mounted volunteers, was also ordered to join me with his company, upon the arrival of Captain Burgwin.

Leaving Lieutenant Colonel Willock in command of this post, on the 23d of January I marched from this place at the head of companies D, Captain McMillen, K, Captain Williams, L, Captain Slack, M, Captain Halley, and N, Captain Barber, of the 2d regiment Missouri mounted volunteers, Captain Angney's battalion of infantry, and a company of Santa Fe volunteers, commanded by Captain St. Vrain. I also took with me four mounted howitzers, which I placed under the command of Lieutenant A. B. Dyer, of the ordnance. My whole force composed three hundred and fifty-three rank and file, and with the exception of Captain St. Vrain's company, were all dismounted. On the march, Captain Williams was taken sick, and the command of company K devolved upon Lieutenant B. F. White. On the 24th of January, at half-past one, p.m., our advance (Captain St. Vrain's company) discovered the enemy in considerable force near the town of Cañada, their position at that time being in the valley bordering the Rio del Norte. Preparations were immediately made by me to attack them; and it became necessary for the troops to march more rapidly than the ammunition and provisions wagons could travel, in order to prevent the escape of the enemy, or to frustrate them in any attempt they might make to occupy commanding positions. As I entered the valley, I discovered them beyond the creek on which the town is situated, and in full possession of the heights commanding the road to Cañada, and of three strong houses at the bases of the hills. My line of battle was immediately formed—the artillery, consisting of four 12-pounder mountain howitzers, being thrown forward on the left flank and beyond the creek, the dismounted men occupying a position where they would be, in some degree, protected by the high bluff bank of the stream from the fire of the enemy, until the wagon train could be brought up. The artillery opened on the houses occupied by the enemy, and on the more distant height, on which alone the guns could be brought to bear.

The enemy discovering the wagons to be more than a mile in the rear sent a large party to cut them off, and it became necessary to detach Captain St. Vrain's company for their protection. This service was rendered in the most satisfactory manner. As soon as the wagon train had been brought up, I ordered Captain Angney to charge with his battalion of infantry, and dislodge the enemy from the house opposite the right flank, and from which a warm fire was being poured on us; this was done in the most gallant manner. A charge was then ordered to be made upon all the points occupied by the enemy in any force. Captain Angney with his command, supported by Lieutenant White's company, charged up one hill, while Captain St. Vrain's company turned the same in order to cut off the enemy when in retreat. The artillery, supported by Captains McMillen, Barber, and Slack, with their respective companies, at the same time took possession of some houses (inclosed by a strong corral densely wooded with fruit trees, from which a brisk fire was kept up by the enemy) and of the heights beyond them. Captain Halley's company was ordered to support Captain Angney. In a few minutes my troops had dislodged the enemy at all points, and they were flying in every direction. The nature of the ground rendered pursuit hopeless, and it being near night I ordered the troops to take up quarters in the town. The number of the enemy were about 1,500. Lieutenant Irvine was wounded. In the charge my loss was 2 killed and 6 wounded—of the killed one was a teamster who volunteered in Captain Angney's company. The loss of the enemy was 36 killed; wounded not ascertained.

47

The next morning the enemy showed themselves in some force (I think not less than 400) on the distant heights. Leaving a strong guard in the town, I marched in pursuit of them; but they were so shy and retreated so rapidly that, finding it impossible to get near them, I returned to town. While at Cañada a number of the horses belonging to Captain Slack's company were brought in by Lieutenant Holcomb.

On the 27th I advanced up to Rio del Morte as far as Luceras, where, early on the 28th, I was joined by Captain Burgwin, commanding Company G, First Dragoons, and Company A, Second Regiment Missouri Mounted Volunteers, commanded by Lieutenant Boone. Captain Burgwin's command was dismounted, and great credit is due to him and his officers and men for the rapidity with which a march so long and arduous was performed. At the same time Lieutenant Wilson, First Dragoons, who had volunteered his services, came up with a 6-pounder which had been sent for from Cañada.

My whole force now comprised 479, rank and file. On the 29th I marched to La Ioya, where I learned that a party of 60 or 80 of the enemy had posted themselves on the steep slopes of the mountains which rise on each side of the canyon or gorge which leads to Embudo. Finding the road by Embudo impracticable for artillery or wagons I detached Captain Burgwin in that direction with his own company dragoons and the companies commanded by Captain St. Vrain and Lieutenant White. This detachment comprised 180, rank and file.

By my permission Adjt. R. Walker, Second Regiment Missouri Mounted Volunteers, accompanied Captain Burgwin. Lieutenant Wilson, 1st dragoons, also volunteered his services as a private in Captain St. Vrain's company.

Captain Burgwin, pushing forward, discovered the enemy, to the number of between six and seven hundred, posted on the sides of the mountains, just where the gorge becomes so contracted as scarcely to admit of the passage of three men marching abreast.

The rapid slopes of the mountains rendered the enemy's position very strong, and its strength was increased by the dense masses of cedar and large fragments of rock which every where offered them shelter. The action was commenced by Captain St. Vrain, who, dismounting his men, ascended the mountain on the left, doing much execution. Flanking parties were thrown out on either side, commanded respectively by Lieutenant White, 2d regiment Missouri mounted volunteers, and Lieutenants McIlvaine and Taylor, 1st dragoons. These parties ascended the hills rapidly, and the enemy soon began to retire in the direction of Embudo, bounding along the steep and rugged sides of the mountains with a speed that defied pursuit. The firing at the pass of Embudo had been heard at La Joya, and Captain Slack, with twenty-five mounted men, had been immediately despatched thither. He now arrived and rendered excellent service by relieving Lieutenant White, whose men were much fatigued. Lieutenants McIlvaine and Taylor were also recalled; and Lieutenant Ingalls was directed to lead a flanking party on the right slope, while Captain Slack performed the same duty on the left. The enemy having by this time retreated beyond our reach, Captain Burgwin marched through the defile, and debouching into the open valley in which Embudo is situated, recalled the flanking parties, and entered that town without opposition, several persons meeting him with a white flag.

Our loss in this action was one man killed, and one severely wounded, both belonging to Captain St. Vrain's company. The loss of the enemy was about twenty killed and sixty wounded.

Thus ended the battle of the pass of Embudo.

On the 30th, Captain Burgwin marched to Trampas, where he was directed to await the arrival of the main body, which, on account of the artillery and wagons, was forced to pursue a more southern route. On the 31st I reached Trampas, and being joined by Capt. Burgwin, marched on to Chamisal with the whole command. On the 1st of February, we reached the summit of the Taos mountain, which was covered with snow to the depth of two feet; and on the 2d, quartered at a small village called Rio Chicito, in the entrance of the valley of Taos. The marches of the 1st and 2d were through deep snow. Many of the men were frost-bitten, and all were very much jaded with the exertions necessary to travel over unbeaten roads, being marched in front of the artillery and wagons in order to break a road through the snow. The constancy and patience with which the troops bore these hardships, deserve all commendation, and cannot be excelled by the most veteran soldiers. On the 3d, I marched through Don Fernando de Taos, and finding that the enemy had fortified themselves in the Pueblo de Taos, proceeded to that place. I found it a place of great strength, being surrounded by adobe walls and strong pickets. Within the enclosure and near the northern and southern walls, arose two large buildings of irregular pyramidal form to the height of seven or eight stories. Each of these buildings was capable of sheltering five or six hundred men. Besides these, there were many smaller buildings, and the large church of the town was situated in the northwestern angle, a small passage being left between it and the outer wall. The exterior wall and all the enclosed buildings were pierced for rifles. The town was admirably calculated for defence, every point of the exterior walls and pickets being flanked by some projecting building as will be seen from the enclosed drawing.

After having reconnoitered the town, I selected the western flank of the church as the point of attack; and about 2 o'clock, p.m., Lieutenant Dyer was ordered to open his battery at the distance of about 250 yards. A fire was kept up by the 6-pounder and the howitzers for about two hours and a half, when, as the ammunition wagon had not yet come up, and the troops were suffering from cold and fatigue, I returned to Don Fernando. Early on the morning of the 4th, I again advanced upon Pueblo. Posting the dragoons under Captain Burgwin about 260 yards from the western flank of the church, I ordered the mounted men under Captains St. Vrain and Slack to a position on the opposite side of the town whence they could discover and intercept any fugitives who might attempt to escape towards the mountains, or in the direction of Don Fernando. The residue of the troops took ground about 300 yards from the northern wall. Here, too, Lieutenant Dyer established himself with the 6-pounder and two howitzers, while Lieutenant Hassandaubel, of Major Clark's battalion light artillery, remained with Captain Burgwin, in command of two howitzers. By this arrangement a cross-fire was obtained, sweeping the front and eastern flank of the church.

All these arrangements having been made, the batteries opened upon the town at nine o'clock, a.m. At 11 o'clock, finding it impossible to breach the walls of the church with the 6-pounder and howitzers, I determined to storm that building. At a signal Capt. Burgwin, at the head of his own company, and that of Captain McMillen, charged the western flank of the church, while Captain Angney, infantry battalion, and Captain Barber and Lieutenant Boon, 2d regiment Missouri mounted volunteers, charged the northern wall. As soon as the troops above mentioned had established themselves under the western wall of the church, axes were used in the attempt to breach it; and, a temporary ladder having been made, the roof was fired. About this time Captain Burgwin, at the head of a small party, left the cover afforded by the flank of the church, and

Colonel Sterling Price
(Dunn, *Massacres of the Mountains*, 1886)

penetrating into the corral in front of that building endeavored to force the door. In this exposed situation, Captain Burgwin received a severe wound which deprived me of his valuable services, and of which he died on the 7th instant. Lieutenant McIlvaine, 1st United States dragoons, and Royall and Lackland 2d regiment mounted volunteers, accompanied Captain Burgwin into the corral; but the attempt on the church door proved fruitless, and they were compelled to retire behind the wall. In the meantime small holes had been cut into the western wall, and shells were thrown in by hand, doing good execution. The 6-pounder was now brought around by Lieutenant Wilson, who at the distance of two hundred yards, poured a heavy fire of grape into the town. The enemy during all this time kept up a destructive fire upon our troops. About half-past three o'clock the 6-pounder was run up within sixty yards of the church, and after ten rounds, one of the holes which had been cut with the axes was widened into a practicable breach. The gun was now run up within ten yards of the wall—a shell was thrown in—three rounds of grape were poured into the breach. The storming party—among whom were Lieutenant Dyer of the ordnance, and Lieutenants Wilson and Taylor 1st dragoons, entered and took possession of the church without opposition. The interior was filled with dense smoke, but for which circumstance our storming party would have suffered great loss. A few of the enemy were seen in the gallery where an open door admitted the air, but they retired without firing a gun. The troops left to support the battery on the north were now ordered to charge on that side. The enemy abandoned the western part of the town. Many took refuge in the large houses on the east, while others endeavored to escape toward the mountains. These latter were pursued by the mounted men under Captains Slack and St. Vrain, who killed fifty-one of them, only two or three men escaping. It was now night, and our troops were quietly quartered in the houses which the enemy had abandoned. On the next morning the enemy sued for peace, and thinking the severe loss they had sustained would prove a salutary lesson, I granted their supplication, on the condition that they should deliver up to me Tomas—one of their principal men, who had instigated and been actively engaged in the murder of Governor Bent and others. The number of the enemy at the battle of Pueblo de Taos was between six and seven hundred. Of these, about one hundred and fifty were killed—wounded not known. Our own loss was seven killed and forty-five wounded. Many of the wounded have since died.

The principal leaders in this insurrection were Tafoya, Pablo Chavis, Pablo Montoya, Cortez, and Tomas, a Pueblo Indian. Of these, Tafoya was killed at Cañada; Chavis was killed at Pueblo; Montoya was hanged at Don Fernando on the 7th instant, and Tomas was shot by a private while in the guard-room at the latter town. Cortez is still at large. This person was at the head of the rebels in the valley of the Mora. For the operations in that quarter I refer you to the subjoined letters from Captains Hendley, separate battalion Missouri mounted volunteers, and Murphy, of the infantry, and Lieutenant McKamey, second regiment Missouri mounted volunteers.

In the battles of Cañada, Embudo, and Pueblo de Taos, the officers and men behaved admirably. Where all conducted themselves gallantly, I consider it improper to distinguish individuals, as such discrimination might operate prejudicially against the just claims of others.

20. WOLDEMAR FISCHER TO THE ADJUTANT GENERAL

SANTA FE, *February 16, 1847.*

SIR:

In obedience to the order of my superior officer, Maj. Lewis M. Clark, commanding the battalion of Missouri Light Artillery, to inform you in his absence from this place of all interesting events which may transpire here, and in which the part of his battalion, stationed at Santa Fe, under my command, may participate, I avail myself of this opportunity to address a few lines to you.

In the last warlike events in New Mexico, from the 23rd of January to the 11th of February last, 26 men of said battalion, under the command of Lieut. F. Hassendeubel, of my company, and Lieutenant Deyer, of the Regular Army, took such a share as will do great honor to the battalion to which they belong. In the first fight at Cañada, on the 24th of January last, the artillery alone was exposed to the fire of the enemy for nearly two hours, which was so effective as to wound 5 men out of 20, and with the exception of one man, all had their clothes perforated by bullets. But they all stood like walls and behaved with such coolness and valor as if they had been veterans and not volunteers, hearing for the first time in their lives the bullets of the enemy whistling by. The same soldier-like and laudable spirit animated them in the next two fights before Pueblo de Taos, where three of them were wounded.

This Pueblo de Taos is one of the most remarkable places in New Mexico, and I take the liberty to add hereto a plan of the same drawn by Lieutenant Hassendeubel at the very place. The two largest buildings are seven stories high; the base covers nearly an acre, and the walls are from 4 to 6 feet thick. The entrance to these houses is from above, and the interior of this labyrinth, as I may call it, is divided and partitioned off in innumerable small rooms, it is believed in nearly three hundred.

The structure of the houses in New Mexico is such as to make the use of mortars necessary that will throw a shell of at least 50 pounds. The walls are generally 3 feet thick and built of "adobes," a sort of sun-dried brick of a very soft quality through which a ball of a 12-pounder will pass without doing any more damage, which in houses of brick or stone is quite different.

I desired very much to participate in these fights myself, but the orders of Colonel Price detained me here in Santa Fe, and when at last an order arrived commanding me to join Colonel Price with 50 men and a 24-pounder howitzer, and I had already started, a counter order reached me on the march commanding me to return to Santa Fe, as Pueblo de Taos was taken and the enemy had surrendered.

I reposed full confidence in my men, when sending them off to fight the battles of their country, that they would conduct themselves as soldiers and men of honor, and, according to the testimony of all officers who were present in this campaign, they have so distinguished themselves by their courage and good discipline as to exceed my just expectations. A great deal of praise is due to Lieutenant Hassendeubel, who, by his brave conduct and his coolness, set a worthy example to the men under his command. I have, sir, the honor to sign myself your most obedient and humble servant,

WOLDEMAR FISCHER,
Captain, Commanding Company B, Missouri Light Artillery, and Commander of Fort Maroy.
Brig. Gen. R. JONES,
Adjutant-General, U. S. A.

21. RUFUS INGALLS TO C. WHARTON

DON FERNANDO DE TAOS, N. MEX., *February 16, 1847.*

COLONEL:
I have the honor herewith to transmit the monthly return of the late Capt. I. H. K. Burgwin's company (G, First Dragoons) for the month of January, 1847.

I have signed the return myself, and in order to explain it beg leave to submit the following statement.

On January 23 Captain Burgwin marched with his company from Albuquerque, a town on the Rio Grande, 70 miles distant from Santa Fe to join Colonel Price. He reached the latter place on January 26. On 28th he joined Colonel Price with his company at a town on the Rio Arriba, 35 miles from Santa Fe in the direction of Taos.

On the 29th he was sent forward in command of a detachment made up of his own company and about 100 volunteers, to drive the enemy from a stronghold in a mountain pass near a town called Embudo. Early in the day Captain Burgwin found the enemy posted on the heights in the ravines and behind all trees and rocks where shelter could be found. The enemy numbered about 500, consisting of Mexicans and Pueblo Indians. Captain Burgwin at once engaged the enemy by ordering Captain St. Vrain's company of citizens and mountain men to dismount and skirmish on the left of the road.

At the same time I was ordered to throw out the dragoons on the right and left. The action lasted about two and one-half hours. The enemy was put to flight with considerable loss and was pursued more than 2 miles from hill to hill through the ravines, and was completely routed and driven beyond the town of Embudo, of which Captain Burgwin took possession and in which his command camped on the night of 29th. In this engagement Captain Burgwin lost 1 man killed and 1 wounded. The enemy lost, so far as could be ascertained, about 20 killed and 60 wounded.

On January 30 Captain Burgwin joined Colonel Price at a town called Trampas, 15 miles from Embudo. On 31st the

Captain James Burgwin
(Frost, *History of New Mexico and Ute Wars*, 1882)

march was continued toward Taos Valley, which Colonel Price reached on the evening of February 2 with his command. On the evening of 3d a march of 6 miles was made to the Pueblo de Taos.

After an attempt to reduce the place by a bombardment it was found impracticable, and Colonel Price returned to Don Fernando de Taos for the night. Early on the morning of 4th the town of Pueblo de Taos, in which the enemy to the number of 1,000 was fortified, was attacked at different points by the artillery and musketeers.

At about 11 o'clock a.m. Captain Burgwin, in command of his own company and a part of Captain McMillins's company, Missouri Volunteers, charged the town from the front and carried by storm all outward defenses up to the walls of the church. A simultaneous charge was to have been made on the left flank by a portion of the large force of volunteers stationed there beyond effective rifle range, but from some mistake the dragoons were first in the charging and for some time were exposed to the galling fire of the enemy through loopholes in the church and main buildings. It was during this period that Captain Burgwin received a mortal wound. The main force, however, coming up soon, carried the church and put many of the enemy to flight. The town was carried and the battle closed near night, having killed about 150 of the enemy.

I assumed command of the dragoons, being the next officer in rank and having served with them in all the engagements.

Capt. I. H. K. Burgwin died on the morning of February 7. In the action of the 4th Company G, First Dragoons, lost 7 killed and 16 wounded, exclusive of the captain.

I am, sir, very respectfully, your most obedient servant,

RUFUS INGALLS,
Second Lieutenant, First Dragoons.
Lieut. Col. C. WHARTON,
Commanding First Dragoons, Fort Leavenworth, Mo.

A true copy.
W. H. STANTON,
Second Lieutenant, First Dragoons.

Then, placing himself at the head of his army, four hundred strong, General Price marched toward Taos. On arriving at Canjarra, a small town about twenty miles from Santa Fé, we found the enemy, numbering two thousand Mexicans and Indians, were prepared to give us battle. The enemy's lines were first perceived by our advanced guard, which instantly fell back upon the main body. Our line was formed, and an advance made upon the enemy, the mountaineer company, under Captain Saverine, being placed in charge of the baggage. As soon as battle was begun, however, we left the baggage and ammunition wagons to take care of themselves, and made a descent upon the foe. He fled precipitately before the charge of our lines, and we encamped upon the field of battle. The next day we advanced to Lamboda, where the enemy made another stand, and again fled on our approach. We marched on until we arrived at Taos, and the barbarities we witnessed there exceeded in brutality all my previous experience with the Indians. Bodies of our murdered fellow-countrymen were lying about the streets, mutilated and disfigured in every possible way, and the hogs and dogs were making a repast upon the remains. Among the dead we recognized that of Governor Bent, who had been recently appointed by General Kearney. One poor victim we saw, who had been stripped naked, scalped alive, and his eyes punched out: he was groping his way through the streets, beseeching some one to shoot him out of his misery, while his inhuman Mexican tormentors were deriving the greatest amusement from the exhibition. Such scenes of unexampled barbarity filled our soldiers' breasts with abhorrence: they became tiger-like in their craving for revenge. Our general directed the desecrated remains to be gathered together, and a guard to be placed over them, while he marched on with his army in pursuit of the barbarians.

Late in the afternoon we arrived at Pueblo, where we found the enemy well posted, having an adobe fort in their front. No attack was attempted that evening, and strict orders were issued for no man to venture out of camp.

In the evening I was visited by a man, who informed me

that he had a brother at Rio Mondo, twelve miles distant, whom, if he was not already killed, he wished to save from massacre. I determined to rescue him, if possible, and, having induced seven other good and trusty mountaineers to aid me in the attempt, we left the camp unperceived, and proceeded to the place indicated. On our arrival we found two or three hundred Mexicans, all well armed; we rode boldly past them and they dispersed, many of them going to their homes. We reached the door of the Mexican general Montaja, who styled himself the "Santa Anna of the North," and captured him. We then liberated the prisoner we were in quest of, and returned to Taos with our captive general. At Taos we found our forces, which had retired upon that place from Pueblo, after having made an unsuccessful attempt to dislodge the enemy. We informed our general of our important capture, and he affected great displeasure at our disobedience of orders, although it was easy to see that, in his eyes, the end had justified the means. The following morning a gallows was erected, and Montaja was swung in the wind. The correspondence that had been seized in Santa Fé had implicated him in some of the blackest plots, and we thought that this summary disposal of his generalship would relieve us from all further danger from his machinations.

Having procured artillery to bombard the enemy's position, our commander returned to Pueblo. We cannonaded in good earnest, but the pieces were too small to be of much service; but we cut a breach with our axes half way through the six-foot wall, and then finished the work with our cannon. While engaged in this novel way of getting at the enemy, a shell was thrown from a mortar at the fort; but our artillerymen, not being very skilful in their practice, threw the shell outside the fort, and it fell among us. A young lieutenant seized it in his hands, and cast it through the breach; it had not more than struck before it exploded, doing considerable damage in the fort. We then stormed the breach, which was only big enough to admit one man at a time, and carried the place without difficulty.

The company of mountaineers had fallen back midway between the fort and mountain, in order to pick off any Mexican who should dare to show himself. We killed fifty-four of the defenders as they were endeavouring to escape, upon the person of one of whom, an officer, we found one hundred and sixty doubloons. Some of the enemy fired upon us from a position at one corner of the fort, through loopholes; and while looking about for a covert to get a secure shot at them, we discovered a few of the enemy hidden away in the brush. One of them, an Indian, ran toward us, exclaiming, "Bueno! bueno! me like Americanos." One of our party said, "If you like the Americans, take this sword, and return to the brush, and kill all the men you find there."

He took the proffered sword, and was busy in the brush for a few minutes, and then returned with his sword-blade dripping with gore, saying, "I have killed them."

"Then you ought to die for killing your own people," said the American, and he shot the Indian dead.

The battle lasted through the whole day, and a close watch was set at night to prevent the escape of those yet occupying the fort. The assault was renewed the following morning, and continued during that day also. Toward night several white flags were raised by the enemy, but were immediately shot down by the Americans, who had determined to show no quarter. On the third morning all the women issued from the fort, each bearing a white flag, and kneeled before the general to supplicate for the lives of their surviving friends. The general was prevailed upon, and gave orders to cease firing. The enemy lost severely through their disgraceful cowardice. Our company lost but one man through the whole engagement. Nine of the most prominent conspirators were hanged at Taos, and seven or eight more at Santa Fé. It was about this time that the report reached us of the butchery of Mr. Waldo, with eight or ten other Americans, at the Moro.

23. DICK WOOTTON'S ACCOUNT

The Americans were by no means certain that the entire force of the enemy had gathered at the Pueblo, but half suspected that a force was secreted in the town of Taos. Before going into camp, they made a careful reconnoisance, inspecting every building in the town, to find out who was inside. Where the doors were closed, they were broken down, and a thorough search made of the buildings, but where they stood open, it was taken as a guarantee of a friendly feeling on the part of the occupants, and their residences were not disturbed.

While the soldiers were in camp that night, I made my way down to where they were, along with my four companions, and joining the Santa Fe volunteers, was ready for the storming of the Pueblo, and the fight which was to commence in the morning. It commenced early, and the battle which followed was a bloody one, considering the number of men engaged in it.

It lasted until sundown, and I think we were resisted as stoutly as were the American soldiers upon any battle field of the Mexican war.

We soon drove our enemies out of the pueblo building proper, but their position in La Iglesia de Taos—the old church—was a strong one, and we found it difficult to dislodge them. We had three small howitzers and one six-pound cannon, but the walls of the church were so thick, that the shells from the howitzers would not go through them, and the solid shot from the cannon only made a round hole. As we were short of ammunition, we could not afford to waste any, and for that reason volunteers were called for to breach the walls with axes. This was a hazardous business, as the work had to be done while a hot fire was being kept up from the inside of the building.

Thirty-five of us, however, volunteered to make the attempt, and we gained the cover of the walls with a loss of only three or four men. It took us but a short time to accomplish what we had started out to do, and when a few shells were thrown through the holes we had made, and exploded in the building, they created a fearful havoc. We lighted the fuses, and threw some of these shells into the church with our hands, in order that they might be sure to explode at the proper time and place.

This made it altogether too hot for the besieged party, and bursting open the doors and windows they undertook to make their escape to the mountains. James Q. Quinn, of Illinois, a cousin of Stephen A. Douglas, planted the American flag on the old church, but as the Mexicans were retreating, they stopped long enough to shoot it down.

The last stand made by the insurgents was at the old church. When they were driven out of there, they fled in every direction. Of course we pursued them, and not much quarter was asked or given. There was considerable hand-to-hand fighting, Colonel St. Vrain himself, I remember, engaging in a contest which in spite of the peril of the situation, was amusing. The colonel was riding along with myself and two or three others, who were about to join in a pursuit of one party of fugitives, when he observed an Indian whom he had seen a great many times, and knew very well, lying stretched out on the ground, apparently dead. Knowing that this Indian had taken a prominent part in the massacre, Colonel St. Vrain dismounted, and walked a few feet from where we were, to see whether the red skin was really dead or only shamming. That the latter, and not the former, was the proper diagnosis of the Indian's case, the colonel was soon very thoroughly convinced. He had scarcely reached the side of the apparently dead Indian, when the latter sprang up, and grappling with him, undertook to thrust into his body a long, steel-pointed arrow. Both the Indian and the colonel were large, powerful men, and as each managed to keep the other from using a weapon, a wrestling-match followed the Indian's attack, which, it seemed to me, lasted several minutes before outside help terminated it in the colonel's favor. I sprang to his assistance as soon as I saw the struggle commence, but the Indian managed to keep the colonel between him and me, and was so active in his movements, that I found it difficult to strike a lick which would be sure to hit the right head. I managed after little, however, to deal him a blow with my tomahawk, which had the effect of causing him to relax his hold upon the colonel, and when he stretched out on the ground again, there was no doubt about his being a dead Indian.

We lost thirty-five men out of the comparatively small number we had engaged in this battle, and among them was Captain Burgwin, who was as brave a soldier as I have ever seen on the frontier. We buried him at Taos in a grave by himself, while the other thirty-four men who were killed, were buried side by side in a long trench near where they fell.

Ceran St. Vrain
(Conard, *"Uncle" Dick Wootton*, 1891)

We never knew exactly what the Mexican and Indian loss was, but it must have been in the neighborhood of two hundred.

This battle ended the Taos rebellion, as it is generally called, although the conspirators had their plans laid to bring about a general uprising of Mexicans and Indians in New Mexico, and they evidently thought with this combination of forces, they would be able to drive the Americans out of the territory, and keep them out.

A detachment of soldiers remained at Taos after that, and the work of hunting down and punishing those who had stirred up, and been prominently connected with the insurrection, commenced.

Pablo Montoya and El Tomacito were both captured. El Tomacito, the Indian leader, was placed under guard, and we proposed to give him, along with the rest, a formal trial, but a dragoon by the name of Fitzgerald saved us the trouble. Fitzgerald was allowed to go into the room where the Indian was confined, along with others who wanted to take a look at him. The soldier looked at the savage a few minutes, and then quick as a flash, drew a pistol and shot him in the head, killing him instantly. Fitzgerald then made his escape from the building, and succeeded in getting away out of the country. If he had been caught he would of course have been punished. The Indian deserved to be killed, and would have been hanged anyhow, but we objected to the informal manner of his taking off.

Pablo Montoya was tried and hanged, and twelve others were disposed of in the same way.

They were all tried by drum-head court-martial, and there was no unnecessary delay about reaching the climax of the proceedings. The twelve that I have spoken of above, were hanged at the same time, and dangled from the same pole. I acted as marshal in making arrests under the military authority, and was kept very busy for some days. The only law we had was military law, but that was just what we wanted, and it was not long before order was restored and the rebellion experiment has never been tried there since.

The traders who had been absent from Taos when the massacre occurred, that is, those who lived there, found, upon their return, that their stores had been sacked and burned, and the most of their property destroyed, but they congratulated themselves upon having escaped with their lives, and after the fashion of the pioneers, set about building up other fortunes to take the place of those they had lost.

24. LEWIS GARRARD'S ACCOUNT

The church was the most important, as well as first, feature in the town, from the fact of its having been the principal scene of action in the fierce and sanguinary conflict between *El Norte Americanos* on the one side and the combined forces of the Pueblo Indians and Mexicans on the other.

It (the church) was an adobe building, parallelogram-shaped; high, thick walls, with no openings on the outer one or those facing the yard, save embrasures and loopholes, rudely cut for the occasion—the late battle. The front entrance faced the south; the west and north sides (as I have mentioned, devoid of windows), the open fields toward the Río Grande, the town of San Fernández and the Ranchita.

As this was the culminating point of all the differences between the Americans and the New Mexicans, an account may be essential to a portion of the readers of this narrative, of the origin, progress, and termination of the then pending difficulties; and, while seated on a broken baggage wagon, to the south, and in full view of the town, looking and musing on the devastating effects of war, the requisite information will be succinctly given. —

General Kearney, in command of the "Army of the West," marched to the capital of this province (Santa Fé) and quietly took possession, claiming it as United States territory. By him, the oath of allegiance was administered to many of the inhabitants in *propria persona*; in many cases, the *alcaldes* or mayors of the small towns received it for themselves and people. In this way the province was Americanized; a governor and a complement of judges, attorneys, sheriffs, and other appurtenances and impertinences of even-handed justice appointed; and, as the people appeared to be well contented, it was thought a bloodless conquest had been made, reflecting credit, alike, on the character of the provincials and the Army of the West! Leaving Colonel Price in command of the military force and Governor Bent as the civil head of the territory, Kearney left New Mexico for California, to add fresh laurels to his wreath of victory, taking with him a small armed force. Of the results of this latter expedition all are cognizant.

In New Mexico everything was in a peaceful, prosperous condition, to all outward show; the people traded freely; small foraging and herding parties of American soldiery were everywhere scattered, placing confidence in the inhabitants. It was afterward seen that designing men—artful and learned natives—were busily, insidiously sowing the seeds of discontent among the more ignorant class of the community, more especially the Pueblo Indians. The result was, they soon considered themselves outraged—their lives at stake—their possessions in danger. With inflamed passions, perverted minds, the brutal attack upon Governor Bent was commenced; and, with cries of extermination, they advanced on Santa Fé, receiving constant accessions in their triumphant march. Meanwhile, in other towns massacres were frequent; and the perpetrators of these, joining the main body of insurgents, met Colonel Price in the cañon El Embuda, where they were defeated with a small loss. They rallied in a few miles, and again they were forced to retreat. Colonel Price, marching with his cannon and baggage train over a new-cut road, through deep snows, followed them to the Pueblo de Taos, the place best calculated, in all the valley, for an obstinate resistance. Here the enemy, barricading themselves in the houses, bid defiance to their pursuers; who, coming on them late in the evening, commenced a bombardment with twelve-pound mountain howitzers. But night forced them to withdraw to San Fernández, two miles distant, amid the cries and jeers of the securely posted foe. In the morning, Price, with his command, moved forward in fine order over the intervening plain, first sending Captain St. Vrain, with whom the reader has become fully acquainted, and his troop of volunteers for the occasion, of mountaineers, traders, etc., skilled in Indian warfare, to the fields between the pueblo and the mountain, a half-mile distant, to intercept the retreat. A fire was opened by the howitzers at four hundred yards, and, after some skirmishing by the infantry and Burgwin's command of dragoons, the enemy retreated to the church, from the numerous loopholes of which they poured out a galling fire. The battery was now ordered up within a hundred yards, which had some effect; but the balls striking the tough mud walls did not always penetrate. Burgwin's dismounted men then stormed the front door of the church. After a spirited attack of several minutes, they were repulsed with the loss of their brave leader. The command devolving on Lieutenant McIlvaine, they were ordered to the west side; where, with axes, a breach was cut, through which they entered, several losing their lives. The cannon were run up to the breach—the bursting of the bombs in the small space, in which so many were crowded, caused great destruction of life. "The mingled noise of bursting shells, firearms, the yells of the Americans, and the shrieks of the wounded," says my narrator, an eyewitness, "was most appalling."

A Delaware Indian, "Big Nigger" by name, a keen shot, was the most desperate of the enemy. When the roof was fired and the Americans poured in, he was pursued to the room behind the altar, where he fell, riddled by thirty balls. Many of the foe fled toward the mountain. Captain St. Vrain, with his company, gave many their final quietus. The American loss was seven killed—that of the enemy 150, with a number of prisoners, among them the leader, Montojo, hung the next day by drumhead court martial in the plaza of San Fernández. Others were committed to jail to await a trial by civil law. Colonel Price returned to Santa Fé, leaving a strong force to support the civil authorities in pursuance of their respective duties. To resume the thread of our narrative—

We stood on the spot where fell the gallant Burgwin, the first captain of the first Dragoons, and then passed to the west side, entering the church at the stormers' breach, through which the missiles of death were hurled. We silently paused in the center of the house of Pueblo worship. Above, between the charred and blackened rafters which leaned from their places as if ready to fall on us, could be seen the spotless blue sky of this pure clime—on either side, the lofty walls, perforated by cannon ball and loophole, let in the long lines of uncertain gray light; and strewed and piled about the floor, as on the day of battle, were broken, burnt beams and heaps of adobes. Climbing and jumping over them, we made our way to the altar, now a broken platform, with scarce a sign or vestige of its former use; and in the room behind, we saw where "Big Nigger" and others, after a determined struggle, bravely met their certain fate. Hatcher was acquainted with the Delawares in former years. On emerging into the enclosure, we looked around.

A few half-scared Pueblos walked listlessly about, vacantly staring in a state of dejected gloomy abstraction. And they might well be so. Their *alcalde* dead, their grain and cattle gone, their church in ruins, the flower of the nation slain or under sentence of death, and the rest—with the exception of those in prison—refugees, starving in the mountains. It was truly a scene of desolation. In the strong hope of victory they made no provision for defeat; in the superstitious belief of the protection afforded by the holy Church, they were astounded beyond measure that, in the hour of need, they should be forsaken by their tutelar saint—that *los diablos Americanos* should, within the limits of consecrated ground, trample triumphant, was too much to bear; and, pitiable objects, they fled as if *diablos* from *los regiones infiernos* were after them, in sooth.

The two *casas grande*, or large houses, in which the Pueblos live are worthy of examination, being constructed of adobes—the universal building material—seven stories in height, each story somewhat smaller than the one below it, sloping gently inward—but not terrace-shaped. The mode of egress is at the topmost story. Ladders are used on the outside, from which they descend to the rooms inside. So subject are the Pueblos to attacks from hostile neighbors that they have, from time to time, thus strengthened their habitations; and as the ladders are pulled to the roof in case of danger, they are safe from their enemies' lances and scalp knives; for should an attempt be made at scaling, they would be exposed to the fire of the besieged from loopholes. An engineer might suggest the plan of undermining the soft building; the Indian besiegers, devoid of invention, have yet to try the plan.

As a mode of defense from their common enemy, the Indian, it certainly is admirable; but what fort or foe can withstand the assaults of the energetic Anglo-Saxon, aided by consummate skill and the most destructive engines of war?

The adobe, or sun-dried brick, is, I think, even better than burnt brick, or stone, to resist a bombardment; as the ball either passes through, making but a small hole, or the force is spent against the wall, without shattering the building. In several places where the cannon ball had penetrated three, four, or five inches, it rolled out again without cracking or shattering the wall in the least. Being tenacious and yielding, the mud brick serves as a good bulwark, not capable of being fired, and, in this dry climate, resists the trials of time and rain exceedingly well. Much credit is due the Pueblos de Taos for their determined and manly resistance to what they considered tyranny and for the capital manner in which their fortifications were planned; but, as a matter of course, they were defeated by the Americans. Who could, for a moment, expect anything else?

For years the Pueblo, by reason of fierceness of disposition, has held the balance of power in this district. It was the Pueblo who first revolted, and committed the late outrages—the Pueblo who, several years since, rose in arms, to put every American to death—the Pueblo who has kept this district in a continual ferment; but, at last! at last, he has met his conqueror.

They approach nearer to civilization than any of the nomadic tribes of the west—profess the Roman Catholic religion; which, by reason of ignorance, is mixed with a large share of superstition; submit to civil law under the guidance of an *alcalde*, of *sangre regular*; cultivate the ground; and, in many points, assimilate to the manners and customs of civilized man.

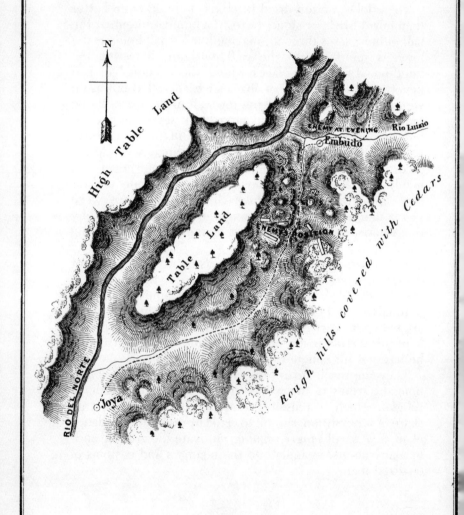

SKETCH accompanying COL. PRICE'S DESPATCH
of 15th Feb. 1847.

The Battle of Embudo
(U.S. Congress, *Insurrection*, 1848)

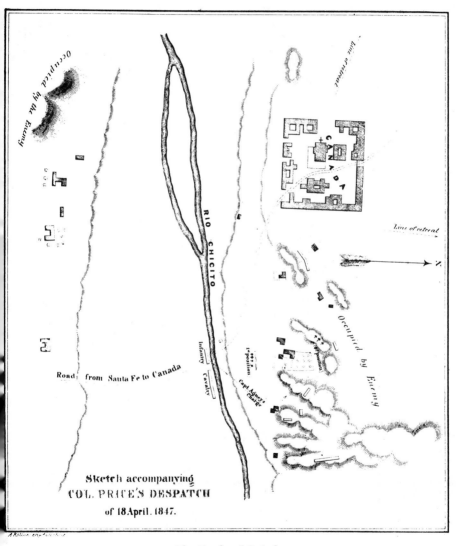

The Battle of Cañada
(U.S. Congress, *Insurrection*, 1848)

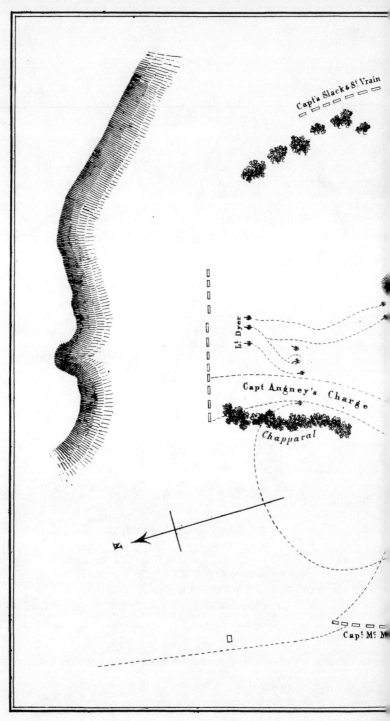

Capt's Slack & St Vrain

Lt Dyer

Capt Angney's Charge

Chapparal

Capt Mc M

The
(U.S. Co

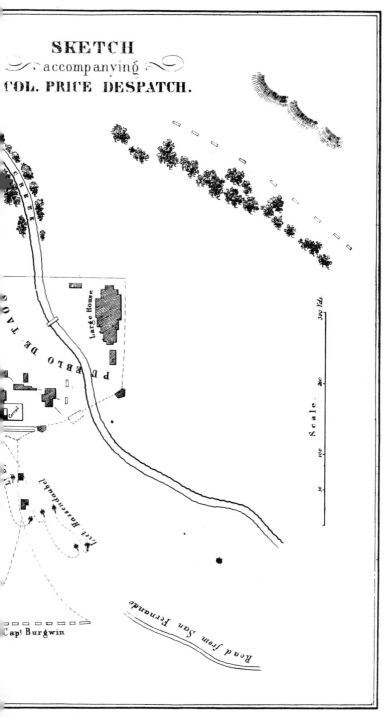

SKETCH
accompanying
COL. PRICE DESPATCH.

CREEK

PUEBLO DE TAOS

Large House

Corral

Pickt Hascendado[es]

Capt Burgwin

Road from San Fernando

Scale.

50   100   200   300 Yds.

VI. Trial and Execution

25. LEWIS GARRARD'S ACCOUNT OF THE TRIAL

Court assembled at nine o'clock. On entering the room, Judges Beaubien and Houghton were occupying their official stations. After many dry preliminaries, six prisoners were brought in—ill-favored, half-scared, sullen fellows; and the jury of Mexicans and Americans—Chadwick, foreman—being empaneled, the trial commenced: F. P. Blair, Jr., prosecuting attorney; assisted by —— Wharton, a great blowhard. The counsel for the defense, whose name I have forgotten, was, as well as Wharton, a volunteer private, on furlough for the occasion. They had, no doubt, joined the ranks in hopes of political preferment on their return home, and the forests of Missouri may yet re-echo with Wharton's stentorian voice, proclaiming to his hero-worshiping constituents how he "fought, bled, and *died*" for his country's liberties—a recapitulation of all the bravado with which many of the military leaders of the discreditable Mexican war have been gulling the "sovereign people" since their return from their easily-won fields of glory.

Mr. St. Vrain was interpreter. When the witnesses (Mexican) touched their lips to the Bible, on taking the oath, it was with such a combination of reverential awe for the Book and fear of *los Americanos* that I could not repress a smile. The poor things were as much frightened as the prisoners at the bar.

It certainly did appear to be a great assumption on the part of the Americans to conquer a country and then arraign the revolting inhabitants for treason. American judges sat on the bench, New Mexicans and Americans filled the jury box, and an American soldiery guarded the halls. Verily, a strange mixture of violence and justice—a strange middle ground between the martial and common law.

After an absence of a few minutes, the jury returned with a verdict of "guilty in the first degree"—five for murder, one for treason. Treason, indeed! What did the poor devil know about his new allegiance? But so it was; and, as the jail was overstocked with others awaiting trial, it was deemed expedient to hasten the execution, and the culprits were sentenced to be hung on the following Friday—hangman's day. When the concluding words "*muerto, muerto, muerto*"—"dead, dead, dead"—were pronounced by Judge Beaubien in his solemn and impressive manner, the painful stillness that reigned in the courtroom and the subdued grief manifested by a few bystanders were noticed not without an inward sympathy. The poor wretches sat with immovable features; but I fancied that under the assumed looks of apathetic indifference could be read the deepest anguish. When remanded to jail till the day of execution, they drew their *sarapes* more closely around them and accompanied the armed guard. I left the room, sick at heart. Justice! Out upon the word, when its distorted meaning is the warrant for murdering those who defend to the last their country and their homes.

Court was in daily session; five more Indians and four Mexicans were sentenced to be hung on the 30th April; but, exciting as were the court proceedings, very few of us spent much time in the room; we wanted to be moving about.

A remarkable circumstance was that whenever Chadwick was on the jury as foreman, the prisoners were returned "guilty in the first degree."

One little Frenchman, Baptiste ——— by name, with not two ideas above eating and drinking, was duly empaneled as a juror, to try the first six subsequently sentenced.

On going into the consulting room, Baptiste went to Chad and asked—"Monsieur Chad*wick*! vot sall I say?" "Keep still man, until we talk awhile to the rest about it," rejoined Chad, "don't be in such a hurry."

"*Oui! oui! eh bien! c'est bon; tres bien! mais Monsieur,* · vot sall ve do *avec sacré prisonniers–sacré enfants—*"

"Baptiste! man, keep still; why, hang them, of course; what did you come in here for?" angrily replied he, much annoyed, "Wait till I am done with these Mexicans [part of the jury], and I will tell you what you must do."

The last cases—the nine just mentioned—Chadwick and
Baptiste were again in their relative positions. As soon as the
jury-room door was closed, he sung out—"Hang 'em, hang
'em, *sacré enfans des garces*, dey dam grand rascale," now
getting excited and pacing the room, *"parceque* dey kill
Monsieur Charles [Governor Bent], dey take *son* topknot,
vot you call im—skulp; *dis enfant*, he go ondare too, *mais*,
he make beevare—run, you Merican say—*pour le mon-
taigne*—wagh! A-ah! *oui*, Monsieur Chadwick, you no tink
so!—hang 'em, hang 'em—*sa-a-cré-é!"*

In the courtroom, on the occasion of the trial of the above
nine prisoners, were Señora Bent, the late governor's wife,
and Señora Boggs, giving in their evidence in regard to the
massacre, of which they were eyewitnesses. Señora Bent
was quite handsome; a few years since, she must have been a
beautiful woman—good figure of her age; luxuriant raven
hair, unexceptionable teeth, and brilliant, dark eyes, the
effect of which was heightened by a clear, brunette
complexion. The other lady, though not so agreeable in
appearance, was much younger. The wife of the renowned
mountaineer Kit Carson also was in attendance. Her style of
beauty was of the haughty, heartbreaking kind—such as
would lead a man with the glance of the eye, to risk his life
for one smile. I could not but desire her acquaintance. The
dress and manners of the three ladies bespoke a greater
degree of refinement than usual.

The courtroom was a small, oblong apartment, dimly
lighted by two narrow windows; a thin railing kept the
bystanders from contact with the functionaries. The
prisoners faced the judges, and the three witnesses (Señoras
Bent, Boggs, and Carson) were close to them on a bench by
the wall. When Mrs. Bent gave in her testimony, the eyes of
the culprits were fixed sternly upon her; on pointing out the
Indian who killed the governor, not a muscle of the chief's
face twitched or betrayed agitation, though he was aware
her evidence unmistakably sealed his death warrant—he sat
with lips gently closed, eyes earnestly centered on her,
without a show of malice or hatred—an almost sublime
spectacle of Indian fortitude and of the severe mastery to
which the emotions can be subjected. Truly, it was a noble
example of Indian stoicism.

26. DONACIANO VIGIL TO JAMES BUCHANAN

SANTA FE, *March, 1847.*

SIR:

Since my letter of the 16th February a number of persons engaged in the late rebellion have been brought to trial before the United States district court for this Territory. Antonio Maria Trujillo was found guilty of treason, and received the sentence of the court.

A petition was immediately laid before me, signed by the presiding justice, one of the associate justices, United States district attorney, the counsel for the defense, most of the members of the jury before whom the accused was tried, and many of the most respectable citizens, praying that the execution of the sentence of the court be suspended until a petition could be laid before the President of the United States for the pardon of the prisoner, on the ground of his age and infirmity.

Though feeling assured that the accused had had a fair trial, and had been justly sentenced and legally convicted, I still feel justified in granting the prayer of the petition, signed as it was by the court and the jury before whom he was tried and convicted.

I am informed that a petition will be immediately forwarded to the President praying for the pardon of Trujillo on the ground above stated. I trust the President will give the matter careful consideration. The prisoner is about 75 years of age, necessarily infirm, and evidently near the end of his days; and, although as the head of an influential family, much was done in his name to excite and forward the late rebellion, still, on account of his years and the near termination of his career, I can not but consider him a proper subject for the mercy of the Government.

The United States district court is still in session at this capital, having under trial three indictments for treason against three prominent persons in the late rebellion. Twenty-four prisoners have been discharged for want of testimony to indict them for treason, and also on the ground that they have been under the influence and deceived by the representations of men who had always exercised tyrannical control over them.

I am informed that there are upward of forty prisoners confined in the northern district awaiting their trial at the coming term of the United States district court for that district.

I can not do less than commend the diligence and at the same time the fairness and justice with which the tribunals of the Territory discharge their duties.

With the highest sentiments of esteem, truly, your obedient servant,

DONACIANO VIGIL.

Hon. JAMES BUCHANAN,
Secretary of State, United States.

27. LEWIS GARRARD'S ACCOUNT OF THE EXECUTIONS

On Friday, the ninth, the sky was unspotted, save by hastily-fleeting clouds; and, as the rising sun loomed over the Taos Mountain, the bright rays, shining on the yellow and white mud houses, reflected cheerful hues, while the shades of the toppling peaks receding from the plain beneath drew within themselves. The humble valley wore an air of calm repose. The plaza was deserted; woe-begone donkeys drawled forth sacreligious brays as the warm sunbeams roused them from hard, grassless ground to scent among straw or bones their breakfast: a *señora* in her nightdress and disheveled hair—which, at the *fandango*, was the admiration of the moustached *señors* and half-wild *voluntarios*—could here and there be seen at this early hour, opening her house, previous to the preparation of the fiery *chile colorado*.

As onward sped the day, so did the crowd of morning drinkers at Estis's tavern renew their libations to Bacchus. Poor Mexicans hurried to and fro casting suspicious glances around; *los Yankees* at *El casa Americàno* drank their juleps and puffed their cigarillos in silence.

The sheriff (Metcalfe, formerly a mountaineer, son-in-law to Estis) was in want of the wherewith to hang the criminals, so he borrowed our rawhide lariats and two or three hempen picket cords of a teamster. In a room adjoining the bar, we put the hangman's noose on one end, tugging away quite heartily.

A while after we had been talking of the propriety, etc., of taking the Mexicans' lives, said Hatcher—"This hos has feelin's hyar," slapping his breast, "for poor human natur in most any fix, but for these palous [*pelados*] he doesn't care a cuss."

"Yes," replied I, "they scalped Liel alive, and butchered innocent persons."

"This coon," remarked Hatcher, "has made Injuns 'go under,' some—wagh!—but he's never skulped 'em alive; this child's no niggur, an' he says its onhuman—agin natur—an' they ought to choke. Hello, Met, these riatas mity stiff—won't fit; eh, old feller?"

"I've got something to *make* 'em fit—good 'intment—don't ermit very sweet parfume; but good 'nough for greasers; freeze into it, boys," said Metcalfe, producing a rial's worth of Mexican soft soap, "this'ill mak 'em slip easy—a long ways too easy for them, I 'spect."

We rubbed in the "'intment" until the nooses could have been "warranted" to serve the intended purpose without hitching; on the teamster's hard ropes, we used an unusual quantity. One item in Met's bill of expenses, was:

"To soft soap for greasing nooses, ... 12½."

Our fee for loan of lariats consisted in the proffered *aguardiente* produced after washing our hands—not of the pleasant transaction of tying hangman's nooses—but of the soap sticking to our fingers.

With newly-lighted cigarillos between our teeth, we walked with the sheriff to the jail, taking along the halters—the significant loops, conspicuous, drawing the attention of both soldier and native, eliciting from the former familiar exclamations, such as—"Go it, my boys," "them's the *doky*ments"—"sarve 'em up brown"—from the latter wondering looks.

Entering a portal with a nod to the sentinel on duty, we found ourselves in a court. In a room fronting this was a ragged, ill-looking *pelado*, conversing with a miserably-dressed old woman—his mother—and discussing greenish-blue *tortillas* and *chile colorado*, under the espionage of a slouchingly-attired, long-haired, dirty, and awkward volunteer, who, to judge by his outward show, was no credit to his corps or silver-gild eagle buttons. He leaned in a most unsoldier-like position against the door frame; and, on our near approach, drew his feet somewhat closer to perpendicular, accosting us with—"Well, strangers! how are ye?"

"Quite well, thank you," replied one of us.

"Them's great briches of yourn," broke in he abruptly, after eyeing my fringed buckskins for some moments, "whar d' they rignate—Santy Fee? Beats linsey-woolsey all holler, down to Callaway County."

"Santa Fé!" replied Hatcher, disgusted with the fellow's simplicity, "why hos, them's Californy!"

"Cal-y-for-ny! my oh! let's look at them, stranger. Calyforny! way over yonder!" halfway soliloquising and staring at me doubtingly, with a side twist to his head and a knowing squint from his porcine eye, "Now, you don't mean to say you was *in* them briches when they was in Calyforny?"

"Him?" interrupted Hatcher, wishing to astonish the man, "that boy's been everywhar. He's stole more mule flesh from the Spaniards an 'raised' more Injun har than you could tuck in your belt in a week!"

"How raise Injine hair? Like we raise corn and hemp to Callaway County, ur jest like raising hogs and y'oxens?"

"Oh! you darned fool," retorted Louy Simonds, "a long ways the greenest Ned, we see yet. No!" rejoined he imperatively, "when an Injun's a 'gone beaver,' we take a knife like this," pulling out his long scalp blade, which motion caused the man to open his eyes, "an' ketch hold of the topknot, an' rip skin an all rite off, quicker an' a goat could jump!"

"What's a 'gone beaver,' stranger?" again spoke up our verdant querist.

"Why, whar *was* you brung up, not to know the meanin' of sich terms—we'ud show you round fur a curiosity up in the mountains—let's go, fellers."

We started to another part of the jail, but were stopped by a final question from our brave volunteer to Hatcher— "Stranger! what mout your name be, ef I mout be so free-like?"

"Well, hos!" returned the questioned, "my name *mout* be Bill Williams, or it mout be Rube Herring, or it mout be

John Smith, or it *mout* be Jim Beckwith, but this buffer's called John L. Hatcher, to rendevoo—Wagh!"

We strolled to the room in which were the condemned and other prisoners, to the number of eighty and more. A brass howitzer, the muzzle within four feet of the door, stood always ready to quell a tumult.

It (the prison apartment) was a long, chilly room, badly ventilated by one small window and the open door, through which the sun lit up the earth floor, and through which the poor *pelados* wistfully gazed. Two muscular Mexicans basked in its genial warmth, a tattered and dirty *sarape* interposed between them and the ground. The ends, once fringed, but now nearly clear of pristine ornament, were partly drawn over their breasts, disclosing in the openings of their fancifully-colored shirts—now glazed with filth and faded with perspiration—the bare skin covered with a wilderness of straight black hair. With hands under their heads, in the mass of stringy locks rusty-brown with neglect, and their attenuated smutty fingers coming through, revealing uncut nails, filled with dirt, they returned our looks with an unmeaning stare, and unheedingly received our salutation of—"*Comme la va!*"

These men were the condemned. In two short hours, they hung lifeless on the gallows.

Along the sides of the room, leaning against the walls, were crowded the poor wretches, miserable in dress, miserable in features, miserable feelings—a more disgusting collection of ragged, lousy, greasy, unwashed *pelados* were, probably, never before congregated within so small a space as the jail of Taos.

About nine o'clock, active preparations were made for the execution, and the soldiery mustered. Reverend *padres*, on the solemn mission of administering the "blessed sacrament" and spiritual consolation, in long, black gowns and meek countenances, passed the sentinels.

Lieutenant Colonel Willock, commanding the military, ordered every American under arms. In accordance with the requisition and with a desire to participate in the fight, should there be any (at least not to be helpless), I went for my gun, which had been delivered to one of the household for safekeeping.

Seeing Señora St. Vrain, in my best Spanish, I said to her—

"*Señora! onde esta riflero? cary mucho.*"—"Madam, where is my rifle? I want it very much."

"*Ah! quien sabe señor?*—"Who knows, sir? Care you a great deal for it?" with a smile and shrug of the shoulders, "*Esta*"—"here"—said she, handing it to me; "*Vamos–prento, por el rancheros*"—"Go quick for the *rancheros.*"

"*Si, gracias Señora–adios*"—"Yes, Madame, thanks,— farewell," replied I, touching my battered wool hat.

"*Adios, Señor Americano*"—"Farewell, Sir American ," returned she, tenderly.

On the houses, as I walked to the jail, were women trying to catch a glimpse of the prisoners and soldiers. As I passed by an *azotea*, on which were two acquaintances, one cried out—"*Señor!*"

"*Quien?*"—"What is it?

"*Eh Señor! los rancheros muy diablos, muy tiefas, caraho!*"—"The *rancheros* are very great thieves—great devils!"

"Yes, ladies"; and I passed on with a low bow in acknowledgment of their salutation.

The prison was at the edge of town; no houses intervened between it and the fields to the north. One hundred and fifty yards distant a scaffold of two upright posts and a crossbeam was erected.

At the portal were several *compañeros*, discussing, in a very light way, the "fun," as they termed it, on hand—they almost wishing a rescue would be attempted so as to gratify their propensity for excitement.

The word was passed, at last, that the criminals were coming. Eighteen soldiers received them at the gate, with their muskets at port arms—the six abreast, with the sheriff on the right—nine soldiers on each side. Hatcher, Louy Simonds, Chadwick, myself, and others, eight in all, formed in line a pace behind, as the rear guard, with our trusty mountain rifles at rest in the bended elbow of the left arm, the right hand resting on the stock, to be drawn up to the face, and all ready to fight on our own responsibility at the least intimation of danger.

The poor *pelados* marched slowly, with down-cast eyes,

arms tied behind, and bare heads, with the exception of white cotton caps stuck on the back part, to be pulled over the face as the last ceremony.

The *azoteas*—roofs—in our vicinity, were covered with women and children, to witness the first execution by hanging in the valley of Taos, save that of Montojo, the insurgent leader. No men were near; a few, afar off, stood moodily looking on.

On the flat jail roof was placed a mountain howitzer (the same piece had done the "state some service" at the battle of the pueblo), loaded and ranging the gallows. Near was the complement of men to serve it, one holding in his hand a lighted match.

The two hundred and thirty soldiers (deducting the eighteen forming the guard) were paraded in front of the jail and in sight of the gibbet, so as to secure the prisoners awaiting trial. Lieutenant Colonel Willock, on a handsome charger, from his position commanded a view of the whole.

When within fifteen paces of the gallows, the side guard, filing off to the right and left, formed, at regular distances from each other, three sides of a hollow square; the mountaineers and myself composed the fourth and front side, in full view of the trembling prisoners, who marched up to the tree, under which was a government wagon with two mules attached. The driver and sheriff assisted them in, ranging them on a board, placed across the hinder end, which maintained its balance, as they were six—an even number—two on each extremity and two in the middle. The gallows was so narrow they touched. The ropes, by reason of size and stiffness despite the soaping given them, were adjusted with difficulty; but, through the indefatigable efforts of the sheriff and the lieutenant (who accompanied us from the ranch), all preliminaries were arranged. The former, officiating as deputy sheriff for the occasion, seemed to enjoy the position—but the blue uniform looked sadly out of place on a hangman.

With rifles grounded, we awaited the consummation of the fearful tragedy. No crowd was around to disturb; a death-like stillness reigned. The spectators on the *azoteas* seemed scarcely to move—their eyes directed to the painful sight of the doomed wretches, with harsh halters now circling their necks.

84

The sheriff and assistant sat down; and, succeeding a few moments of intense expectation, the heart-wrung victims said a few words to their people. But one said that they had committed murder and deserved death. In their brief, but earnest appeals, which I could but imperfectly comprehend, the words "*mi padre, mi madre*"—"my father, my mother"—could be distinguished. The one sentenced for *treason* showed a spirit of martyrdom worthy of the cause for which he died—the liberty of his country; and, instead of the cringing, contemptible recantation of the others, his speech was firm asseverations of his own innocence, the unjustness of his trial, and the arbitrary conduct of his murderers. With a scowl, as the cap was pulled over his face, the last words he uttered between his gritting teeth were, "*Caraho, los Americanos!*" The atrocity of the act of hanging that man for treason is most damnable; with the execution of those for murder no fault should be found.

Bidding each other "*adios,*" with a hope of meeting in Heaven, at word from the sheriff the mules were started, and the wagon drawn from under the tree. No fall was given, and their feet remained on the board till the ropes drew taut. The bodies swayed back and forth, and, coming in contact with each other, convulsive shudders shook their frames; the muscles, contracting, would relax, and again contract, and the bodies writhed most horribly.

While thus swinging, the hands of two came together, which they held with a firm grasp till the muscles loosened in death.

After forty minutes suspension, Colonel Willock ordered his command to quarters, and the howitzer was taken from its place on the prison roof. The soldiers were called off; the women, children, and population in general collected around us—the rear guard—whom the sheriff detained for protection while delivering the dead bodies to the weeping relatives.

We made a collection among ourselves of five dollars and dispatched a messenger to *el casa Americano* to prepare for us, when relieved from duty, an eggnog in honor of the occasion, for the Mexican has long been the dislike of the mountaineer, for overbearing conduct. Now that they have, for once, triumphed, a merrymaking must be given. We helped the sheriff to take down the bodies and untie the ropes—a most unpleasant business, too, for the cold, clammy skins and dead weight were revolting to the touch.

We were cutting a rope from one man's neck—it was in such a hard knot—when the owner (a government teamster), standing by waiting, shouted angrily, at the same time starting forward—

"Hello there! Don't cut that rope; I wont have any thing to tie my mules with."

"Oh! you darned fool," interposed a mountaineer, "the palous' ghosts'll be after you, if you use them 'riatas—wagh! They'll make meat of you, sartain."

"Well, I don't care if they do. I'm in government service; an' if them picket halters was gone, slap down would go a dollar apiece. Money's scarce in these diggins, an' I'm gwine to save all I kin, to take home to the old 'oman and the boys."

In accordance with the fellow's earnest request, we spared the ropes, on which was soap enough for a dozen good washings, which he much needed.

VII. Aftermath

28. FROM CHARLES E. MAGOON'S REPORT TO THE SECRETARY OF WAR—1900

In May, 1847, a wagon train and a grazing party were attacked by the insurgents and one or two men killed and a large number of horses and mules captured. Major Edmonson pursued this force and encountered them, nearly 400 strong, in a canyon of the Red River. The American forces engaged them, but after fighting several hours and succeeding in killing and wounding many Mexicans were unable to dislodge the enemy and retired. The next day he found the enemy had fled during the night.

In June, 1847, the insurrection affected Las Vegas. Lieut. R. T. Brown and 3 soldiers were killed. Thereupon Major Edmonson made an attack and killed 10 or 12 men. He also found evidence of a new revolt, and captured the town, sent about 50 citizens as prisoners to Santa Fe, and burned a mill belonging to the alcalde, whom he thought was implicated in the revolt.

In July, 1847, a party of 31 American soldiers was attacked at La Cienega, and Lieutenant Larkin and 5 other men were killed. On the approach of reenforcements the insurgents fled and were not apprehended.

During the month (July, 1847) Major Edmonson is said to have destroyed the town of Las Pias, with considerable loss to the insurgents and to have marched by way of Anton Chico to La Cuesto, where were about 400 insurgents under Cortez. Fifty prisoners were taken, the main body of the enemy escaping into the mountains. (See Bancroft's Arizona and New Mexico, p. 435, Bancroft's Works, vol. 17.)

Thereafter the insurrection dwindled into depredations committed by various bands of Indians, instigated and led by Mexicans. Hardly a party, large or small, traders or soldiers, crossed the plains of New Mexico without being attacked. Many men were killed and large numbers of horses, mules, and cattle driven off. A company of dragoons escorting Government funds lost 5 men killed and all their animals in June.

In the latter part of 1847 comparative safety was secured by stationing troops at various points. Of the insurgent prisoners 15 or 20, perhaps more, were tried by court-martial, sentenced to death, and executed. The others were turned over to the civil authorities of the military government for trial in the civil courts. The grand jury indicted 4 of them. The others were discharged for want of evidence or pardoned by the governor. The 4 indicted were charged with treason against the United States Government. One was tried by a jury and convicted. The prisoner challenged the jurisdiction of the civil court and assailed the indictment on the ground that he was not a citizen of the United States, nor bound to yield allegiance to that Government. Strong pressure was brought to bear in his behalf, and the district attorney, Mr. Blair, referred the matter to Washington for instruction. Mr. Marcy, Secretary of War, advised the President as follows:

On the 26th of June, 1847, I wrote to the commanding officer of Santa Fe a letter (a copy of which accompanies this communication) in which the incorrect description of the crime in the proceedings of the court is pointed out. It is therein stated that "the territory conquered by our arms does not become, by the mere act of conquest, a permanent part of the United States, and the inhabitants of such territory are not, to the full extent of the term, citizens of the United States. It is beyond dispute that on the establishment of a temporary civil government in a conquered country the inhabitants owe obedience to it and are bound by the laws which may be adopted. They may be tried and punished for offenses. Those in New Mexico who in the late insurrection were guilty of murder, or instigated others to that crime, were liable to be punished for these acts, either by the civil or military authority, but is not the proper use of legal terms to say that their offenses were treason committed against the United States; for to the Government of the United States—as the Government under our Constitution—it would not be correct to say that they owed allegiance. It appears by the letter of Mr. Blair, to which I have referred, that those engaged in the insurrection have been proceeded against as traitors to the United States. In this respect I think there was error, so far as relates to the designation of the offense. Their offense was against the temporary civil government of New Mexico and the laws provided for it, which that government had the right and, indeed, was bound to see executed."

For this reason the President declined to exercise the power to pardon vested in him as the chief civil magistrate of the United States, but, as commander in chief of the Army, authorized the military governor to use his discretion in the matter, and the prisoner was pardoned by the governor.

The events resulting from this insurrection did not escape the attention of Congress. That body, on July 10, 1848, passed a resolution calling upon the President for information in regard to the existence of civil governments in New Mexico and California; their form and character, by whom instituted and by what authority, and how they were maintained and supported; also whether any persons had been tried and condemned for "treason against the United States" in New Mexico.

President Polk replied to said resolution by message (dated July 17) received July 24, 1848, in which he discusses the character of military government, taking the position that such a government may exercise the "fullest rights of sovereignty." (See Ex. Doc. No. 70, first session Thirtieth Congress.)

The official documents, copies of which and extracts from which are herewith presented, are much more interesting than this inadequate sketch of their contents.

Respectfully submitted.

29. DONACIANO VIGIL TO JAMES BUCHANAN

SANTA FE, *March 26, 1847.*

SIR:

A few days since the colonel commanding received a deputation of principal men from the Navajo Indians, from whom he exacted a promise that all the prisoners and stock taken in their late marauding expeditions against the settlements of the southern district should be restored by the end of the present month.

I have no confidence of the fulfillment of the promise indeed, these Indians continue to commit daily outrage in the disregard of their promise. I hope measures will be immediately taken by the officer in command here to compel not only a restitution of property and prisoners, but to secure for the future respect for our arms and Government, and a lasting submission on the part of these turbulent savages. The interest and prosperity of the Territory urgently demands it.

In the late attacks of these Indians many citizens have been deprived of their all, and unless something be speedily done to prevent further depredations, the native citizens will have just cause to complain that the promises made to them by Brigadier-General Kearny, to the effect that they should be protected against these Indians, their ancient enemies, has been shamefully violated and disregarded.

It is with feelings of the highest gratification that I am able to announce that Col. A. W. Doniphan entered the city of Chihuahua on the 1st instant, having met the enemy on the day previous at Sacramento, some 18 miles from the city, upward of 4,000 strong, and in an action of three hours, with his command of 1,400 men, including the wagoners of the merchants' caravans, gained a victory almost unprecedented in history, putting the enemy to flight, leaving 169 dead on the field, while the command lost only 2 killed and 7 wounded.

I can not close without again urging upon the Government the absolute necessity of replacing the present volunteer force in this territory by a force of Regular troops, on the ground of greater economy, expediency, and efficiency. In my opinion, both the interests of the United States and of this Territory clearly demand it.

With sentiments of the highest esteem, truly, your obedient servant,

DONACIANO VIGIL.

Hon. JAMES BUCHANAN,
  Secretary of State of the United States.

30. D. B. Edmonson to Sterling Price

CAMP NEAR SANTA CLARA SPRINGS, NEW MEXICO,
June 14, 1847.

SIR:

In compliance with Orders, No. 187, May 16, I proceeded to Las Vegas with Companies B and F, Second Regiment Missouri Mounted Volunteers, and the detachment Laclede Rangers, commanded by Lieutenant Elliott. Upon my arrival at San Magil I was informed that a large party of Shian and Apache Indians had gone to the mouth of the Moro on Red River to join a marauding party of Mexicans and others, numbering 300 to 400, and commanded by the outlaw Cortes, and that small detachments were being sent into the settlements to commit depredations on the property of the citizens and American soldiers. On my arrival at Las Vegas, May 20, being informed that a party of about 50 Indians were in the mountains 30 miles north, having with them about 200 stolen animals, I dispatched Company F, Captain Horine, in pursuit. On the same day Company B, Captain Dent, was sent to disperse a marauding party said to be about 40 miles south of this place.

On the evening of the same day I received information of the surprise of our grazing party under Captain Roberson near Wagon Mound by a party of Indians and Mexicans, in which we lost 1 man killed and 2 wounded, and about 250 horses. Being destitute of mounted men in consequence of the departure of the commands of Captains Horine and Dent on the morning previous, I immediately ordered in the grazing parties from the Ocato. I was thus enabled by the use of some Government animals to mount between 75 and 80 men, with which command I reached Captain Roberson's camp on the evening of the 24th. I there found Captain Brown (with 12 wagons laden with goods belonging to our settlers, Messrs. Rich and Pomroy), who had been attacked the previous day at Santa Clara Springs (8 miles distant) by the Indians, who made a desperate effort to get possession of the wagons. Failing in that attempt, they drove his oxen out of reach of gunshot and deliberately killed them to the number of between 60 and 70. The killing of the cattle was doubtless intended to detain the wagons and thus afford an opportunity to surprise and get possession of them. On the following morning, 25th, leaving about 30 men for the protection of the settler's wagons, I organized two scouting parties, one under charge of Captain Holoway and the other under charge of Lieutenant Elliot, with direction to rendezvous at Santa Clara Springs the following night. We that day discovered where the enemy had corralled their animals a few days previous in the mountains about 15 miles south of Santa Clara Springs, but had left in the direction of Red River. On the following morning, after forming an advance or spy party, under command of Captain Holoway, Company E, the remainder were formed into three platoons; No. 1, commanded by Captain Roberson; No. 2, by Lieutenant Elliot, and No. 3 by Lieutenant Brown, Company F. Thus organized, I proceeded to follow the trail discovered on the day previous to the canyon of Red River. I entered it with Captain Roberson's command, leaving the commands of Lieutenants Elliot and Brown behind, the company of spies going some fifty minutes in advance in order to prevent surprise. Descending into the canyon with great difficulty through the rocks, leading our horses and following the meanderings of the Indian trail about half a mile, I discovered three Indians secreted behind the rocks about 200 yards from our trail. Supposing that a large number might be there secreted, and having myself the advantage of the ground, I ordered a halt until the rear of the command should arrive. Whereupon the three Indians, who had no doubt been placed there as sentinels, made a rush for their horses, they being close at hand and ready saddled. They were immediately fired upon, killing one of them and unhorsing another; the two remaining Indians mounted one horse and thus made their escape for the time. We then continued to descend to the bottom of the canyon, and with some difficulty effected a crossing of the river. Pursuing the tracks up the bank of the river, we passed the two Indians above spoken of, who immediately made a desperate attempt to reach the main body of the enemy, who were then in our rear, but were immediately pursued and both slain before they could reach their party. The hills around us were by this time literally covered with Indians and Mexicans, who witnessed the tragedy and opened fire upon us from every point occupied by them. The bottom of the canyon was so narrow as to expose our men to the fire of the enemy from the hills on either side, which were very rocky and so nearly perpendicular as to render a charge impossible. I determined to recross the river in view of occupying some high points on the opposite side which would at all times command the outlet from the canyon, but the enemy, understanding the order, or anticipating it, got possession of the ford before the men could be rallied, who were somewhat scattered in the pursuit of the two Indians spoken of.

I then returned up the river some half mile and took possession of a point of rocks which was out of gunshot reach from the hills on the opposite side of the river, but being too far from the river to command access to water, I determined to occupy a point more favorably situated, in passing to which Lieutenants Elliot, Miller, and Sursey, who were in the rear, discovered a large party of Mexicans rapidly descending the hill (who had escaped my notice), rallied about 20 men and kept them in check until the main body got possession of the point last designated. The men were immediately ordered to dismount, conceal their horses as far as possible, and take advantage of the rocks until the enemy should approach sufficiently near to enable us to make a charge, sending at the same time a detachment to the bank of the river to secure the water and prevent the enemy passing up the canyon in our rear. Our troops being thus disposed of, the fight commenced at the three several points and continued without intermisson about four hours, the enemy alternately advancing and retreating as new recruits arrived.

About sunset, having driven beyond our reach the Indians and Mexicans, finding a large portion of the troops out of ammunition, many of our men having ceased firing for want of it, and knowing that we would necessarily have to fight our way out of the canyon, as the enemy occupied the passes, I determined to reach the open ground at the top of the canyon before dark, which was effected in good order, except in fording the river, where the enemy, anticipating our movement, were concealed in considerable numbers, opened a hot fire, wounding two of our men and killing several horses. After crossing the river we returned the fire of the Indians and drove them back with the loss of 5 killed and several wounded. We then proceeded to the top of the hill in good order, reaching it at dark, whereupon our troops were immediately formed for action; but no enemy appearing, we marched to water and encamped for the night, in view of returning to the canyon the following morning. Our number in the engagement was 77. The number of the enemy could not be correctly ascertained, but have been variously estimated at from 400 to 600. Our loss was 1 man killed and 3 slightly wounded, while the enemy's loss was reported at 41 killed. The number of their wounded could not be ascertained, as they were removed off the field as fast as they fell.

On consulting with the officers the next day, 27th, and finding that portion of our troops furnished by the grazing parties (composing much the largest portion of the command) were entirely out of ammunition, we were reluctantly compelled to suspend operations until a further supply could be obtained. Upon reentering the canyon we found that the enemy had left on the night after the battle in great haste, leaving horses, cattle, camp equipage, etc., not taking time to scalp or strip our man lost in the action, as is their custom. We pursued them with all possible dispatch to their first camping ground in their retreat, where from appearances, they had made a division of their property and forces. We continued to follow their traces many miles in the plains, until, getting among large herds of mustangs or wild horses, it became impossible to track them farther. Our horses being much fatigued and tenderfooted from our travel over the rocks, we returned to our present camp near Wagon Mound. Since the 26th of May (as far as my knowledge extends) there has been no further depredations committed in or marauding parties infesting this portion of the Territory.

Respectfully, yours, etc.,

D. B. Edmonson,
Major, Commanding Detachment, etc.

Col. Price,
Commanding Army in New Mexico.

31. STERLING PRICE TO THE ADJUTANT GENERAL

HEADQUARTERS NINTH MILITARY DEPARTMENT,
Santa Fe, July 20, 1847.

SIR:

Since the insurrection of January and February last, a body of Mexicans and Indians, embodied for predatory purposes, have been very annoying along the line of the eastern settlements of this Territory, where many of our grazing camps were established. They did not, however, venture an attack upon any of the detachments in that quarter until the 20th of May last, when the camp of Captain Robinson, separate battalion, Missouri Mounted Volunteers, was surprised, and about 200 horses and mules were driven off. In this affair Captain Robinson lost 1 man killed and 2 wounded.

Information of these events was immediately sent to Major Edmonson, commanding at Vegas, who at once marched in pursuit of the marauders whom he found on the 26th June in a deep canyon on the Rio Colorado, or more properly, the Canadian River.

Major Edmonson entered the canyon and a desultory fight ensued, for the particulars of which I refer you to the official report of engagement, which is herewith sent. This unsuccessful attempt to recapture the lost animals has emboldened the Mexicans and Indians to commit further acts of aggression. On June 27 Lieut. R. T. Brown, Second Missouri Mounted Volunteers, with 2 volunteers and a Mexican guide started in pursuit of some horses which had been stolen at Vegas. Lieutenant Brown found the animals at Las Vallas, a small village about 15 miles south of Vegas, but upon his seizing them, the Mexicans resisted and murdered the whole party. As soon as Major Edmonson was informed of the massacre of this party he marched from Vegas, and, surprising the town, shot down a few who attempted to escape and took about 40 prisoners. These prisoners are now confined in this city awaiting their trial.

On the 6th of July the grazing camp of Captain Morin's company (Separate Battalion Missouri Mounted Volunteers) was attacked, Lieutenant Larkin and 4 men were killed and 9 wounded, and all the horses, besides property of every description, fell into the hands of the outlaws. Lieutenant-Colonel Willock, commanding at Taos, immediately marched in pursuit of them, but at length, finding it impossible to overtake them, returned to Taos.

The forces under my command are now so much diminished by the departure of the companies whose terms of service have expired, that I consider it necessary to concentrate my whole command at this city. Rumors of insurrections are rife, and it is said that a large force is approaching from the direction of Chihuahua. I am unable to determine whether these rumors are true or false, but it is certain that the New Mexicans entertain deadly hatred against the Americans, and that they will cut off small parties of the latter whenever they think they can escape detection.

General Orders, No. 14, have been received and promulgated, and it is probable that three or four companies, composed of discharged volunteers and teamsters, formerly in the employment of the assistant quartermaster, may be mustered into the service of the United States at this city.

I have the honor to be, very respectfully, your obedient servant,

STERLING PRICE,
Colonel, Commanding the Ninth Military Department.
THE ADJUTANT-GENERAL OF THE ARMY,
Washington, D. C.

VIII. Biographical Sketches

Jim Beckwourth (1800?-1866?)

Son of a minor Irish aristocrat and a mulatto slave woman. Beckwourth led a long and colorful life as a fur trader and scout. One of the more famous mountain men, he was also one of the most notorious story tellers on the frontier. In 1854 he told his life story to Thomas Bonner who brought out the *Life and Adventures of James P. Beckwourth*. Long thought to be a collection of tall tales—or more impolitely, a pack of lies—much of what Beckwourth told Bonner has been verified from other sources. Still, while many of the incidents related by the mountain man are fairly accurate, there is no doubt that he consistently exaggerated his role in them.

Charles Bent (1799-1847)

The eldest of the Bent brothers, Charles founded "Bent, St. Vrain and Company" with Ceran St. Vrain in 1830. The company built Bent's Fort in 1833 as a post for trade with the Indians and became the largest trading organization in the southwest. In the 1830s Bent moved to Taos where he married Maria Ignacia Jaramillo. His involvement in the factional New Mexican politics and his trade with the enemies of the Pueblo Indians made him an obvious target when the revolt broke out.

Hector Lewis Garrard (1829-1887)

In 1846, as a young man of seventeen, Hector Lewis Garrard set out from his parents' home in Cincinnati for a "vacation" in the West. He joined Ceran St. Vrain's caravan at Westport and enthusiastically adopted the life and ways of a trader, traveling among the Indians and living at Bent's Fort. He eagerly joined a small expedition to Taos at word of the murders there. On his way home to Ohio he enlisted in the garrison of Fort Mann in order to add Indian fighting to his experiences.

Garrard was an extraordinary observer, and his book, *Wah-to-yah and the Taos Trail*, published in 1850 under the name of Lewis H. Garrard, is an invaluable source for the history of the Taos Revolt and of life on the plains in the late 1840s. When he died at fifty-eight he could look back on a full and satisfying life in the midwest, but it is for his adventures as a teen-ager and his superb book recounting them that he is remembered today.

Sterling Price (1809-1867)

Born in Virginia, Price migrated to Missouri with his parents in 1831. He served three terms in the Missouri General Assembly and was elected to the U.S. Congress in 1844. He lost the nomination two years later and resigned to take the appointment as colonel of the 2nd Missouri Mounted Volunteers, raised for the invasion of New Mexico. He acquitted himself well in the Taos Revolt and ended the war with the rank of brevet brigadier general.

After the Mexican War he returned to his tobacco plantation and politics. As a result of his proslavery stand he was elected governor of Missouri in 1852. He opposed secession in 1860-61 but accepted command of the Missouri state guard in 1861 and defeated Union forces at Wilson's Creek and Lexington. In 1862 he received a commission in the Confederate army but had little success at the head of regular troops. After a year and a half exile in Mexico following the war he returned to St. Louis to try his hand at business. His health broken by the rigors of war, he died shortly thereafter.

Dick Wootton (1816-1893)

In his later years a famous Coloarado pioneer, Wootton began his western career at the age of twenty as an employee of Bent and St. Vrain's company. With other mountain men he went on a two year trapping expedition in 1838 that took him over most of the central Rockies and the Northwest. After playing his part in the Taos Revolt he joined Colonel Doniphan in Chihuahua in time to participate in the Battle of Sacramento. He later acted as an army scout, drove sheep to California, ran a blacksmith shop near Pueblo, established a trading post in Denver to serve the gold hunters and built a toll road over Raton Pass. One of the most versatile of westerners, he lived long enough to enjoy being a legend in his own time.

IX. Bibliography

BOOKS

Bancroft, Hubert Howe. *History of Arizona and New Mexico, 1530-1888*. San Francisco: The History Company, 1889.

Bauer, K. Jack. *The Mexican War, 1846-1848*. New York: Macmillan, 1974.

Beck, Warren A. *New Mexico: A History of Four Centuries*. Norman: University of Oklahoma Press, 1962.

Beckwourth, James P. *The Life and Adventures of James P. Beckwourth*. New York: Harper and Brothers, 1856.

Conard, Howard Lewis. *"Uncle Dick" Wootton*. Chicago: W.E. Dribble & Co., 1890.

Garrard, Lewis H. *Wah-to-yah and the Taos Trail*. Cincinnati: W.H. Derby & Co., 1850.

Johnson, Abraham Robinson, Marcellus Ball Edwards and Philip Gooch Ferguson. *Marching with the Army of the West*. Ed. by Ralph P. Bieber. Glendale: Arthur H. Clark, 1936.

Lamar, Howard P., ed. *The Reader's Encyclopedia of the American West*. New York: Thomas Y. Crowell, 1977.

Lavender, David. *Bent's Fort*. Lincoln: University of Nebraska Press, 1954.

Ruxton, G.F. *Adventures in Mexico and the Rocky Mountains*. London: J. Murray, 1847.

Twitchell, Ralph Emerson. *The History of the Military Occupation of the Territory of New Mexico*. Reprint. Chicago: Rio Grande Press, 1963.

_____. *The Leading Facts of New Mexican History*. Cedar Rapids: Torch Press, 1912.

U.S. Congress. *Insurrection Against the Military Government in New Mexico and California, 1847 and 1848*. Sen. Doc. No. 442, 56th Congress, 1st Sess. Washington: G.P.O., 1900.

Weber, David J. *The Taos Trappers.* Norman: University of Oklahoma Press, 1971.

ARTICLES

Burton, E. Bennett. "The Taos Rebellion." *Old Santa Fe* 1:176-85.
Cheetham, Francis T. "The First Term of the American Court in Taos, New Mexico." *New Mexico Historical Review* 1:23-41
Goodrich, James W. "Revolt at Mora, 1847." *New Mexico Historical Review* 47:49-60.
Murphy, Lawrence R. "The United States Army in Taos, 1847-1852." *New Mexico Historical Review* 47:33-48.
Myers, Lee. "Illinois Volunteers in New Mexico, 1847-1848." *New Mexico Historical Review* 47:5-31.

SOURCES

Beckwourth. *Life and Adventures:* Nos. 8, 22
Conard. *"Uncle Dick" Wootton:* Nos. 4, 9, 23
Garrard. *Wah-to-yah:* Nos. 5, 10, 24, 25, 27
Ruxton. *Adventures: No. 7*
Twitchell. *Leading Facts:* No. 6
U.S. Congress. *Insurrection:* Nos. 1-3, 11-21, 26, 28-31

MICHAEL MCNIERNEY is a free lance writer and editor who specializes in western history. He received his B.A. degree from the University of Colorado and his M. A. from the University of Denver. He has also done graduate work in history at Iowa State University. Mr. McNierney is a long-time resident of Boulder, Colorado.

Johnson Publishing Company   ISBN: 0-933472-07-2/$4.95